The Heads that Fell in Paris

The Heads that Fell in Paris

by
Georges Grison

translated, annotated and introduced by
Freeman G. Henry

A Black Coat Press Book

English adaptation and introduction Copyright © 2016 by Freeman G. Henry.
Cover illustration Copyright © 2016 Daniele Serra.

Visit our website at www.blackcoatpress.com

ISBN 978-1-61227-501-7. First Printing. April 2016. Published by Black Coat Press, an imprint of Hollywood Comics.com, LLC, P.O. Box 17270, Encino, CA 91416. All rights reserved. Except for review purposes, no part of this book may be reproduced or transmitted in any form or by any means, electronic or mechanical, including photocopying, recording, or by any information storage and retrieval system, without permission in writing from the publisher. The stories and characters depicted in this novel are entirely fictional. Printed in the United States of America.

TABLE OF CONTENTS

Introduction 7
THE HEADS THAT FELL IN PARIS 21
APPENDIX 261

Introduction

The Texts
The present text is a translation of Georges Grison's *Souvenirs de la Place de la Roquette*, originally published in Paris in 1883 by the publishing house E. Dentu and included in the series Librairie de la Société des Gens de Lettres. An identical photographic reproduction of the original published by Hachette Livre (BNF) served as the base text. That text is also available on-line at *gallica.bnf.fr*.

Georges Grison and **Le Figaro**
Georges-Édouard-Alexandre-Stanislas Grison, the son of a tax collector, set out for Paris in 1866 to seek his fortune in Paris as a novelist and playwright. He was twenty-five at the time and had worked in the financial sector in his birthplace, Saintes, a historic city located on the banks of the Charente River in southwestern France.

His decision was hardly unique. Paris, as nucleus of the French sensorium (in the words of the nineteenth-century historian Jules Michelet), had been attracting young men of his ilk for generations. In 1866 the attraction proved all the greater, for Baron Haussmann was putting the final touches on his renovation and sanitization of the city that was quickly gaining the reputation as the most beautiful of the world's capitals. His concept of esthetic functionalism included razing slums, excavating broad boulevards to replace dreary, dank, medieval alleyways, and fashioning *ronds-points* (roundabouts) adorned with fountains and flowers, along with the construction of monumental buildings of Renaissance inspiration. The effect was mesmerizing; people relocated to Paris by the droves. The City of Light had become a megalopolis, its numbers expanding well beyond a million.

Young Georges knew he faced an uphill battle. The competition was daunting, especially for someone from the provinces. In order to make ends meet, he took a job in the administrative offices of the Lyon Railway Company. In his spare time, when he was not engrossed in his literary endeavors, he tried his hand at writing articles for various newspapers. What began as a means of supplementing his income and garnering some attention as a writer ultimately turned into a fulltime enterprise.

The exact number of newspapers for which he wrote is impossible to determine. He began by freelancing, of course, and so very often such contributions go unsigned.[1] To gain the foothold necessary to be invited to join the staff at a first-rate newspaper, he certainly had to undergo a trial by fire involving numerous publications. That took time. It was not until after the Franco-Prussian War (in which he was a volunteer) and the Commune that his big break came. Unfortunately for France, but fortunately for him, the hiatus was brief. Up-

---

[1] Angelo de Gubernatis's *Dictionnaire international des écrivains du jour* (Florence: Louis Niccolai, 1890) lists *Le Petit Moniteur* and *La Petite Presse* as newspapers in which Grison debuted (Vol 2, p. 1104).

on his return he was taken on board by *Le Figaro* and spent the next thirty years turning out copy on a regular basis at the expense of his literary projects.[2]

By the 1860s *Le Figaro* (France's longest running newspaper) already had a distinguished if intermittent history. The first version was established in 1826 by Maurice Alhoy and Étienne Arago as an anti-establishment satirical publication. After less than three months the editorship passed into the hands of the novelist Auguste le Poitevin. After six months another author assumed the position of owner-director, Victor Bohain, a playwright and entrepreneur, who hired Nestor Roqueplan as editor in chief and contracted for the services of yet another novelist, Alphonse Karr. After the July Revolution (in which *Le Figaro* played an active role) Henri de Latouche, novelist, playwright, and editor of André Chénier's poetry, joined the team. Soon George Sand and Jules Sandeau were contributing copy. The decided literary bent and talented stable of writers were not enough to prevent the venture from folding in 1835, after a shareholders' revolt and legislation that increased the required operating bond, subjugated all

---

[2] Information concerning *Le Figaro* has been drawn from several sources. Two works by Claire Blandin stand out: *Le Figaro: deux siècles d'histoire*. Paris: Armand Colin, 2007 and a collection of essays under her direction, *Le Figaro: Histoire d'un journal*. Paris: Nouveau Monde, 2010. See also Saint-Vincent, Bertrand and Jean-Charles Chapuzet. *Le roman du Figaro*. Paris: Plon, 2006; *Histoire générale de la presse*, Vol. 2 ("De 1815 à 1871"). Paris: Presses Universitaires de France, 1969; and Henry, Freeman G. "Gautier, Nerval et Alphonse Karr: badinage, esprit et parti pris au *Figaro*." *Bulletin de la Société Théophile Gautier*, 23 (2001), 275-291.

artwork to censorship, and expanded the number of criminal infractions applicable the press.

The following year Alphonse Karr came to the rescue. In order to circumvent government repression, he devised a statement of purpose that prioritized apolitical satire, pleasantries, and abject nonsense, all in the spirit of the comedic genius of Beaumarchais and the eponymous figure of Figaro. Under the guise of harmless banter, the newspaper took to task all of French society and culture, as well as foreign manifestations such as Turkish harems and English snobbism. The required banter did not make for writers of lesser quality, however. To the contrary, under the guise of anonymity Karr drew into his fold some of the most recognizable names of all of French literature: Honoré de Balzac, Alexandre Dumas (père), Eugène Scribe, Gérard de Nerval, and Théophile Gautier.

Prior versions of *Le Figaro* were but a distant memory by the time Grison joined the staff in the early1870s. That did not mean that the tradition established all those years before had been abandoned. Hippolyte de Villemessant took a cue from Alphonse Karr when he relaunched the newspaper in 1854. Like his predecessor, he faced a repressive body of legislation. The laws promulgated in 1852 aimed at muting the political press, but nonpolitical satire of the fashionable lifestyle of Imperial France was fair game. The heritage of quality satire written by quality writers thus resurfaced. While avoiding pedantry, Villemessant sought to cultivate a friendly elitism that would attract discerning readers capable of appreciating all the arts as well as the fine-tuned yet mordant irony that would fill his pages. The literary emphasis continued to obtain, and, over time, would attract the cream of the crop: Francisque Sarcey, Jules Vallès, Charles Baudelaire, Émile Zola.

Villemessant's innovations were crowned by his elevation of *Le Figaro* to daily status in November of 1866. He had already commercialized his operations by attracting investors, and in1867 he created *Le Petit Figaro* as an alternative to the very successful *Le Petit Journal*. In it appeared short stories, accounts of tribunals, serial novels, the "now playing" of the Paris theatrical scene, and so on. This was where readers would find many of Grison's contributions. At the same time, for the parent *Le Figaro*, political and other sensitive topics no longer needed to be avoided. There was, however, a strict, nonpartisan policy and an aura of objectivity that made its pages the place where perceptive readers could find–beyond fashion and fine literature–unblemished, factual accounts of the happenings of the day. (Grison never tired of saying that in his columns he related only what he witnessed personally, leaving speculation to others.)

Villemessant's vision was so successful that by 1874 the offices of *Le Figaro* were housed at 26 Rue Drouot in a grandiose building of stunning baroque architecture that included a dispatch room worthy of a museum. There, illustrations, engravings, and, eventually, photographs of current events were available for public viewing. Such was the ambiance into which Grison was drawn. He would not leave for decades.

Grison was one of the reporters assigned the metropolitan crime beat. If Haussmann had made Paris a model city, there remained plenty of misdeeds to go around. In fact, it can be argued that by razing low-rent quarters, his grandiose plans increased poverty and edged borderline criminals into the mainstream. In addition, Grison was selected to cover calamities and anything macabre, including executions. Though increasingly reduced in number, executions were far from uncommon. The guillotine, adopted during the French Revolution, became the mainstay means to that end. Indeed, it would endure until 1977.

If these multifarious assignments kept Grison on the run, they did not keep him completely from his literary calling. As in the case of *Souvenirs de la Place de la Roquette*, those assignments often nurtured his writings. Being on the spot at crime scenes, in courtrooms, at accidents, and at executions provided a unique vantage point from which to tell his tales. The press and the literary arts enjoyed a symbiotic relationship in nineteenth century France. As noted, journalists were often fine novelists and poets in their own right. That made for scintillating prose and certainly added a meaningful dimension to the commercial prospects of any newspaper. What was more, the poetry and serial novels that soon found their way into their pages proved to be a major attraction. If that meant added resources for struggling writers, it also influenced the form of their output. The epic poem did experience a rebirth during those years, but the newspapers had nothing to do with its newly gained success. Epic poetry was far too long for the limited space they could offer in any given issue. Shorter poetry was another matter. The newspapers did play an important role in the rejuvenation of the sonnet whose fourteen lines had fallen out of favor since the sixteenth century. A similar influence occurred with regard to the novel. The novel's length precluded inclusion in its entirety, of course, but snippets, in serial form, that was another matter. Novelists soon began composing their works with the newspapers in mind, episodically, holistically sectioned in order to mime a certain completeness while providing just enough mystery or anticipation to motivate the reader to purchase the issue in which the next installment would appear.

The Bibliothèque Nationale de France attributes some forty literary works to Georges Grison. They may be categorized as novelized current events, sentimental novels, crime stories, tales of the macabre, and theatrical productions (as cowriter).

That total and breadth may seem surprising, but it is somewhat misleading. It took Grison some time to get his literary legs. The first two publications listed, *Paris horrible & Paris original* (*Horrible Paris & Original Paris*) and *Les accidents de Chemins de fer, grandes catastrophes* (*Railway Accidents, Great Catastrophes*), carry the date 1882, that is, sixteen years after Grison's arrival in Paris and a full decade after he had been taken on by *Le Figaro*. A number of the titles, though published, are listed as "inédit," meaning they had been composed some time before and published belatedly. Others exist only in manuscript form, for there is no indication of publication dates or publishers. Most of the titles were published from the 1890s up to 1927, the year before his death.

Whatever literary notoriety Grison enjoyed, then, came largely in his later years.[3] It appears that 1888 was

---

[3] There is evidence of current interest in Grison's works. Two titles, *Souvenirs de la Place de la Roquette* and *Paris horrible & Paris original*, have been made available on-line recently. Additionally, Nathalie Prince included a Grison narrative in her fascinating anthology *Petit musée des horreurs. Nouvelles fantastiques, cruelles et macabres* (Paris: Laffont, 2008). The

a key year in that sense. That was the year that Henry Vizetelly, the celebrated, London-born author, editor, publisher, and entrepreneur, opted to include in his anthology *French Sensational Novels* a translation of Grison's *13, rue des Chantres (au 2e étage). Célérité et discrétion* (1885). The English language version, *Dispatch and Secrecy* (taken from the subtitle), places Grison in very good company, indeed. Vizetelly was known for publishing translations of the works of many of the finest writers of the day, Flaubert, Daudet, Gogol, Dostoyevsky, Tolstoy, among others.

Jean de Paris, Monsieur de Paris, and The Place de la Roquette

When Grison signed his articles, he often used the name Jean de Paris. It would seem that his pen name had nothing to do with the thirteenth-century, liberal-thinking cleric Jean Quidort/Johannes de Soardis who used the same pseudonym. Neither does there seem to be any link with the anonymous, fifteenth-century *Le roman de Jean de Paris*, a history in praise of Charles VIII that was republished in the nineteenth century. The most plausible explanation lies in its homonym: Gens de Paris (the people of Paris). Whatever the case may be, there is a glaring link to a character who appears repeatedly in Grison's articles and, especially, in *Souvenirs de la Place de la Roquette*: Monsieur de Paris, the sobriquet applied to the individual bearing the title of Chief Executioner of France. Because of their professions, Jean de Paris and Monsieur de Paris were destined to rub shoul-

---

piece, *Les violateurs de sépultures* (*Tomb Raiders*) appeared originally in *Le Figaro* in 1886.

ders for an entire decade. Over time they became fast friends.

Souvenirs de la Place de la Roquette (here translated as *The Heads That Fell in Paris*) is an edited and expanded compilation of the series of articles Grison wrote for *Le Figaro* as the newspaper's man on the scene at executions from 1872 to 1882. The original title references the spacious square in the eleventh arrondissement where executions were held. Bordering it were two prisons, La Petite Roquette, a facility housing young offenders, and La Grande Roquette, a larger facility for detainees scheduled to be executed or deported. La Grande Roquette could accommodate some four hundred fifty prisoners in its two hundred fifty cells and several dormitories. There was also a common ground within the walls to which designated prisoners had access during the day. La Grande Roquette was inaugurated in 1836. Along with it came a change in venue of the official execution site, which had been located at the Barrière de Saint-Jacques in the fourteenth arrondissement. Both facilities endured until 1974 when they were pulled down.

Form and Content

Grison's text is divided into chapters sandwiched by an introduction and a conclusion calling not only for an extension of the death penalty, but also a reduction in the number of commutations that had been on the increase for several years. The death penalty had been openly contested throughout the century. With the fall of the Second Empire, proponents of its abolition were buoyed by the return from voluntary exile of their most vocal supporter: Victor Hugo. Grison took exception.

The question is hardly out of date today. Whereas it is true that the European Union has banned capital punishment both for peace-time crimes and for war crimes, it persists today in many parts of the world, some of them otherwise lauded for their stance on human rights. The reader will recognize in Grison's argumentation many of the points that are reiterated today in its defense.

A brief history of the guillotine follows the introduction. It is of interest not only because it reflects an effort to orient the reader historically, but also because it references the enormous corpus of tales, legends, and songs devoted to the terrible machine. It had become ingrained in popular culture, and Grison's depiction helps explain why executions continued to attract droves of spectators from every walk of life.

Before turning to individual executions, Grison introduces the chief executioner with whom he dealt for most of his ten years on the beat, Nicolas Roch. He outlines his rise from the rank of executioner's aide to the top of his profession, a profession shared by his father and uncle. (One is put in mind of the English film "The Last Hangman.") In an effort to furnish statistical documentation, Grison provides a list of all of Roch's eighty-odd executions, followed by a tabulation of the ever-decreasing executions in France from 1800 to the time of the writing, 1883, once again, in support of his stance on the death penalty.

The eyewitness accounts begin with Chapter Four, the execution of Jean-Baptiste Moreux. All of the executions detailed by Grison resulted from murders. Accompanying factors differ greatly, however. Mutilations, dismemberments, bludgeonings, rapes, pedophilia, necrophilia, parricide, the gamut proves to be hideously extensive. Along the way changes in the penal code are brought to light. Torture was abolished in 1810, as was, in 1832, the amputation of the right hand of a person convicted of parricide. By 1850 the penalty for counterfeiting had been reduced to forced labor, and the death penalty for arson was rarely invoked.

True to his word involving accuracy and straightforward reporting, Grison does not indulge in the ghoulish for its own sake. There is plenty of blood and gore, but they are presented more in line with a crime report than a spine-chiller. Too, his depictions of the executions themselves become, let's say, somewhat repetitious. The reason for that is two-fold. First, Grison was turning his individual journalistic accounts into a book. In each article he had been careful to name all of the figurants in each execution in the interest of documenting the event as precisely as possible and, surely, to gain whatever advantage citing the individual names of officials might garner him in the future. Moreover, seeking a quick turnaround in publication, he was not of a mind to rewrite extensively. Second, the law mandated a specific protocol, ceremonial in character, almost theatrical: the waking of the prisoner, the words of compassion from the prison's chaplain, physical preparation of the prisoner (cutting of hair, cutting of shirt collar, the application of restraints), the ride and/or walk to the scaffold, and the execution itself, down to the thudding of the head into a basket, transportation of the body to the cemetery for burial, and final prayers at graveside.

Admittedly, some of the descriptions of the crowd reaction wear thin. Spectators and reporters alike always seem to shudder at the same point in each execution, for example. Such repetitions are less than felicitous. Moreover, Grison is not always consistent or accurate in reporting dates of executions. Reference to the public registry of executions is included in the footnotes in order to reorient the reader. The discerning reader will sometimes be puzzled by the development of a case. Whereas the crime investigation and the teamwork of police and investigating magistrates are strong points in general, from time to time hiatuses and non sequiturs weaken the account.

That said, there is much to admire in the work. It provides an unabashed, insider's view of a divisive practice that continues to this day. In doing so, Grison shows an admirable respect for each condemned person as a human being. Furthermore, in the interest of science, he sometimes follows a cadaver into the medical laboratories of the Paris School of Medicine where he describes in minute detail and using specific anatomical terminology the dissection and experiments doctors performed following the execution. If occasionally repetitious, Grison can also be esthetically pleasing, especially when it comes to descriptions of the countryside or the area surrounding the execution site. In Chapter Seven, Grison depicts a serene setting in stark contrast to the event he is on his way to witness.

"At a spot called Porte Morard, the road ran above a large body of placid water. As though a platinum mirror, its surface, bathed completely in moonlight, reflected perfectly the tall, shimmering poplars, the small, charming houses that might have been out of a comic opera, a mill that awaited daybreak to resume its tic toc, and, farther along, the age-roughened, lacelike gable of a house built in 1350. In the distance, on a dark green hillside dotted with copses, other houses of varying sizes and periods could be seen, interspaced here and there by the silhouettes of small steeples. A poet with any Germanic sensitivity at all would certainly have been moved to see the Wilis passionately dancing above the trees or over the melancholic expanse of water."

In Chapter Thirty-Two the execution site itself provides the wherewithal to wax poetic.

"The execution site had taken on a forebodingly sinister aura. The rain had stopped, but flashes of lightning continued to streak across the sky, illuminating in violent, ghostly fashion the tall, black walls of the two prisons, the area surrounding the five granite slabs, and the weapons of the various contingents of troops that arrived the one after the other. All that, the tall denuded walls, the colossal, gray gate through which the prisoner would emerge, the horses, the cavaliers wrapped in their large coats, all that stood out in dazzling silhouettes for just an instant and then fell back into a dense darkness in which only the red glow of lanterns coming and going remained."

The Appendix

Chapters Twenty-Three to Twenty-Five are devoted to a case that drew international attention and sparked keen debate in both England and the United States. Whereas Grison covers the physical crime and investigation in detail, his primary interest in the case deals with the postmortem dissection of and experimentation on Aimé Barré's body. For others, the motivation of the second murderer, Paul Lebiez, was paramount. Lebiez, a medical student who dissected and dismembered the body of an aging female milk vendor, attributed the crime to his understanding of Charles Darwin's theory of the survival of the fittest and his reading of Dostoyevsky's *Crime and Punishment*. The execution, which caused a frenzy in Paris, attracted some thirty thousand spectators to the Place de la Roquette. The appendix contains excerpts of an account of the crime published thirteen years later, three articles describing events drawn from London newspapers and published in the *New York Times*, as well as a police report describing the execution itself.

Freeman G. Henry

THE HEADS THAT FELL IN PARIS

CHAPTER ONE
History, Legends, and Songs of the Guillotine

The death penalty in France has been abolished, in practice if not in law. A jury, in its wisdom, has recently seen fit to grant a verdict of mitigating circumstances to Messieurs Gilles and Abadie, those two young thugs who marauded about the countryside killing and plundering as they went and had the audacity to laugh and brag about their exploits to anyone foolish enough to listen. Other juries have reached similar conclusions, sparing the lives of shameless murderers: that sniveling cretin Fallois, for example, who went to the Rue Fontaine-au-Roi in the eleventh arrondissement, robbed and killed his employer, and skipped off to Alsace where he thought he could safely lead a foppish life simply by crossing the border; or that monstrous, ungrateful student named Bistor who strangled his friend's grandmother with her dog's leash, even though the kindhearted woman had helped him out of numerous difficulties and had loved him like a son; or indeed that Monsieur Fenayrou, the sportsman and pharmacist who had invented both a patented hair tonic and also an unpatented, yet highly creative use for a lead-weighted rope.

After due consideration, one can only conclude that these juries have done their job all too well. Yet had they not been so clement, the President of the Republic would have commuted their sentences. Staunchly opposed to the death penalty, Monsieur Grévy [4] has recently granted clemency to a long list of some of the most despicable characters the earth has ever seen. One had stomped his father to death because the old man hadn't obliged him by dying sooner. Another was a highwayman who compounded theft with rampant murder. Another still had disemboweled a little girl. Their sentences were commuted, every one!

I have nothing more to add. I must yield to the most-worthy decisions of the first magistrate of the land. Nevertheless, the effect is obviously the abolition of capital punishment. Henceforth, the guillotine may as well be dismantled and placed in a museum as a curiosity of a bygone era.

What I can do, however, is to preserve the memory of its contribution to the history of France by presenting an eyewitness account of the most recent executions.

For those of you who say executions are all alike and of little interest, I beg to differ. For eleven years I was assigned to cover more than twenty of them as a matter of professional responsibility. I can assure you that on each occasion I observed a distinct, moving scene that left me with a wide range of impressions. Without fail, as it played out and for a variety of reasons, each lugubrious ceremony took on a special character all its own.

During all those years I noted one sole invariable: not once did it rain the night of an execution, a coincidence strange but true. Other than that common point, no two executions were alike. You will surely be convinced

---

[4] Jules Grévy served as third president of the Third Republic from 1879 to 1887, following Adolphe Thiers (1871-73) and Patrice de Mac-Mahon (1873-79).

of it if you take the time to read the succeeding accounts which, whatever their merit, have the virtue of being absolutely accurate. I wrote each one the very morning following the execution upon returning either from the Place de la Roquette or from the provinces where the sentence was carried out. I did so with the emotions aroused by the drama still fresh in my mind and despite being exhausted from the rigors of a night spent out of doors. For the sake of accuracy, I hurriedly jotted down my impressions as they occurred to me without endeavoring to structure them and without rereading them for fear of reliving the gruesome spectacle of the victim's convulsing body and his grimacing head falling into the wicker basket.

It is at the request of my cohorts at *Le Figaro* that I have decided to publish these accounts on their own. They assure me that the interest they generated individually in the newspaper will be even greater when they appear together in a single volume. It is with that thought in mind that I have undertaken the project.

Before sharing with you the experience of the first execution I attended, it occurs to me that I should say a few words about the instrument used today by executioners and which has been completely modified over the years.

The *Guillotine*, to call it by its proper name, is not a proper noun as such. Contrary to legend, Doctor Guillotin–my compatriot whose granddaughters are presently school teachers near Saintes–was neither the inventor nor the first victim of the death-dealing device.[5]

---

[5] Joseph Ignace Guillotin (1738-1814). Grison had lived in Paris for many years, but he obviously kept in touch with

The guillotine has a much lengthier history than commonly believed. The chronicler Jean d'Anton, who died in 1528, reports its use in his chronicles published for the first time in 1835 by Monsieur Paul Lacroix, also known as P. L. Jacob, Bibliophile. Recounting an execution that took place in Genoa the 13th of May 1507 (while Louis XII was visiting the city), he writes that Demetri Justin, who had induced the people to revolt, was condemned to death. Having arrived at the execution site, "he extended his neck onto the lunette. The executioner took hold of a rope that was attached to a heavy block fitted with a cutting blade and suspended between two poles. He pulled the rope. The blade fell and struck the Genoese between the head and the shoulders in such a way that his head ended up on one side and his body on the other side."

That device was none other than the *mannaja* described at length by Father Labat in his *Voyage en Italie* in 1730 and used to behead Beatrice Cenci in Rome in 1600.[6] The decapitating device is also depicted in two copper engravings, one by Georges Penez (who died in 1550), the other by Henri Aldergrave (dated 1553), as well as in a painting that is reportedly still the property of the city hall in Augsbourg, Germany. Jacob Cats, the very popular Dutch poet, devoted an entire chapter to it in his poem titled *Dootkiste* (*The Coffin*) published in Amsterdam in 1665.

I should also add that the Scots had a similar instrument known as the Maiden that was used to execute

---

friends and family in Saintes, the birthplace he and Guillotin shared.

[6] Biographers list the date of her execution as September 11, 1599.

the Marquis of Argyle (1651) and his son (1685). Finally, it was with such a device that the Duke of Montmorency was decapitated in Toulouse in 1632. "In that land," writes Paységur in his *Memoirs*,[7] "executioners use a teardrop-shaped blade (doloire) supported by two pieces of wood. When the victim's head is placed on the block, the rope is released and the head is separated from the body."

However, although the device was known, it was used only rarely. The rope continued to be used for commoners; the sword or the axe was used for nobles.

It was Doctor Antoine Louis, Secretary of the College of Surgeons, who in 1792 composed the report calling for the adoption of the first guillotine. The first death machine was built by Tobias Schmitz, a piano maker, based on the design by a fellow named Laquiante, a court clerk from Strasbourg. (The first blade had a concave cutting edge. At the request of Louis XVI, a new triangular blade replaced it.)

The guillotine went into action April 25th, 1792. At that date the two immense uprights between which the blade was placed ("the arms of the guillotine," as they were called) rose high above a platform (accessible only by a stairway consisting of twenty-four steps) and were visible from a considerable distance. The entire lugubrious contraption was painted red, not a bright red capable of lifting one's spirits, but rather a dark, brooding red, the color of dried blood.

---

[7] Le Seigneur de Paységur is more commonly known as le Seigneur de Puységur. Armand-Marie-Jacques de Chastenet gained a reputation as a mesmerist and as a proponent of the theory of animal magnetism. His *Memoirs* were published in 1747.

The horror of the device intensifies as the condemned person, already half dead from dread, is escorted to its base. It intensifies further as the prisoner is forced to mount the stairs and is physically prepared to receive the blade before being stretched out and tied to the bascule. Finally, it reaches its apex during the long, agonizing moments waiting for the blade to fall.

This awesome structure that turned executions into public spectacles featuring the executioner, the priest, and the convict was reduced little by little to the height of a man. The platform was reduced in size, as well. The "arms" were able to be lowered by increasing the blade's weight to compensate for the diminution of force and by replacing the original greased grooves that guided the blade's trajectory with a series of pulleys that eliminated friction. The result of these modifications was that the instrument of death could be practically hidden from view by the cordon of mounted gendarmes that surrounded the scaffold. As it exists today, the guillotine stands at ground level, the platform having been eliminated completely. Likewise, it is no longer the color of dried blood. That has been replaced either by a dull green or a dark brown.

At the same time modifications were made to the blade itself whose cutting edge was easily blunted. The idea of using a square blade had to be discarded because it would have required an extremely heavy weight. The instruments presently in use feature an oblique blade that slices angularly and with unfailing efficacy.

With the oblique blade, one need not worry about repeating the horrible scene that Victor Hugo describes in the preface of *Le dernier jour d'un condamné* (*The Last Day of a Condemned Man*, 1829). The executioner of a condemned woman, Hugo writes, so badly bungled the process that after five attempts the blade had still not put an end to her.[8]

One last yet important modification has been introduced. The condemned person is no longer lashed to the bascule. Instead, as the priest is uttering his final words, the victim is seized fiercely and forced headlong onto the plank without warning.

This apparent brutality is in reality an act of kindness, for there is no time for the prisoner to think about what is happening–as it should be, according to Monsieur Nicholas Roch, Chief Executioner of France.

I stated earlier that Doctor Guillotine's name has been wrongly attached to this instrument of death. That association stems from a now-famous utterance he pronounced before the entire Constituent Assembly. In demanding that the death penalty be clemently enacted by a mechanical apparatus rather than a person and in response to those raising objections, he asserted in midsession: "With this machine I can cut your head off in the blink of an eye and you won't feel a thing!"

The result was a chorus of laughter. Those words reverberated far and wide; they were repeated endlessly and were even turned into song:

---

[8] The preface dates from 1832. Grison is mistaken in that the scene involves a man, not a woman. Moreover, as Hugo describes it, it is far more gruesome than Grison lets on. In the narrative, after five blood-spurting attempts, the triangular blade has not managed to completely sever the man's head. At that point the crowd forces the executioner from the scaffold, the man, still conscious, begs for mercy, and an executioner's aide finishes the job with a butcher knife.

Guillotin,	Guillotin,
Médecin	Doctor,
Politique	Politician,
Imagine un beau matin	Imagines one fine morning
Que pendre est inhumain	That hanging is not humane
Et peu patriotique.	And not at all patriotic.
Aussitôt	Therefore
Il lui faut	We need
Un supplice	A penalty
Qui, sans corde ni poteau,	That, with neither rope nor post,
Supprime du bourreau	Eliminates the hangman's
L'office.	Office.
C'est en vain que l'on publie	It is in vain that it is said
Que c'est pure jalousie	To be due to the jealousy
D'un suppôt	Of a flunky
Du tripot	From the club
D'Hippocrate	Of Hippocrates
Qui d'occire impunément,	Who, able to kill guiltlessly
Même exclusivement	And even exclusively,
Se flatte	Flatters himself
Et sa main	And by his hand
Fait soudain	Suddenly appears
La machine	The machine
Qui simplement nous tuera	That purely and simply will kill us
Et que l'on nommera	And whose name shall be
Guillotine.	The Guillotine.

(*Actes des Apôtres*, no. 10)⁹

Another song explains the system:

C'est un coup que l'on reçoit,	It's a blow that's delivered,
Avant qu'on s'en doute;	Before you know it;
A peine on s'en aperçoit	It's hardly even noticed
Car on n'y voit goutte.	For nary a drop is seen.
Tout à coup étant lâché	All of a sudden is released
Un couperet bien caché,	A well-hidden blade that
Fait tomber	Slices away
Ber, ber,	Kachunk,
Fait sauter	Cuts away,
Ter, ter	Kaplunk
Fait tomber, fait voler la tête	And sends the severed head flying.
C'est bien plus honnête!	Now that's surely the better way!

For some time the guillotine was known as the Louison or the Louisette, but that designation failed to endure.¹⁰

Since I'm talking about songs and verses, I'd like to rectify an error or rather a literary prank that has gained credibility over time and that would otherwise become

---

[9] The reference is to a periodical listed by the Bibliothèque Nationale de France as appearing in 1790 and numbering fourteen volumes. I hope the reader will forgive me for not rendering rhymed versions of this and subsequent songs and poetry (FGH).

[10] So called for Doctor Antoine Louis, Secretary of the College of Surgery, who had a hand in its design and approval.

as legendary as the invention of the guillotine. A few years ago there appeared in *Le Figaro* an unpublished bit of poetry by Alfred de Musset and which, it was said, the author of *Rolla* and *Les Nuits* had never intended to publish. It was a sonnet titled *Paysage matinal* (*Morning Landscape*):

Voici l'homme qu'un prêtre amène,	There's the man led by a priest,
Crrrac! Il est déjà "basculé";	Zip! He's already laid out;
La lunette, assez large à peine	The lunette is just large enough
S'abat sur son col étranglé.	To squeeze in his pinched neck.
Poum!... C'est fait. La Justice humaine	Zoom! It's over. Humane justice
A son dû. Le chef décollé	Has been served. The neckless head
Tombe en la cuve demi-pleine	Falls into the tub now half full
De son très peu renouvelé,	Of bran not entirely fresh,
Pendant qu'en un long jet tiède	While in a long, warm stream
Jusque dans l'estomac de l'aide	Against the stomach of the aide
Le sang fumant jaillit du col.	Steaming blood spurts from the neck.
Puis, la tête au panier se verse...	Then, the head drains in the basket...
Satan, penché sur la traverse,	Satan, on the cross-bar perched
Guette l'âme, et la happe au vol.	And on the watch, snatches the soul on the fly.

These lines have been reproduced numerous times and have always appeared under the name of Alfred de Musset. Now, here is the truth of the matter. They were composed in my presence by Gaston Vassy.[11] We even debated for a quarter of an hour whether to attribute them to Musset or to Baudelaire.

---

[11] Gaston Vassy is the pseudonym of Gaston Pérodeaud (1847-1885), a journalist who wrote for both *Le Figaro* and *L'Événement*.

CHAPTER TWO
The Executioners: The One Hundred Seventy-Three Heads of Monsieur Nicholas Roch

I intend to speak only about what I have seen personally. Therefore, my accounts will not date back farther than the tenure of Monsieur Heidenreich, with whom I spent little time. I can say, however, that the man who enjoyed such celebrity status in Paris, as a result of the Troppmann execution, displayed all the trappings of a perfect gentleman.[12]

Six feet in height, cool, calm, clear-eyed, his hair worn in a brush cut, short sideburns, his face otherwise closely shaved, he looked the part of a retired colonel. Monsieur Heidenreich carried out his duties dressed in black with a white tie. After each execution, he went to church where he arranged a special mass for the victim whose life he had been charged with ending. Then, as if to wash away the undesirable remnants, he went for a bath. He could have been, as anyone can see, an executioner out of a novel.

---

[12] Jean-François Heidenreich (1811-1872) served as the first Chief Executioner of the French Republic from 1871 to 1872. Grison's spelling (Heindreich) has been corrected throughout. The Troppmann case ranks as one of the most heinous crimes in nineteenth-century France. Jean-Baptiste Troppmann (1848-1870) was convicted of brutally killing the eight members of the Kink family in Pantin in 1869. His execution attracted throngs of spectators, including the Russian novelist, Ivan Turgenev, who in 1870 published a moving account of it: "The Execution of Troppmann."

And yet people should not be fooled by his calm demeanor. One of my colleagues knows better. I shall not name this person, who is well-known in Paris and who, at the present time, has left journalism for the theater. I'll just limit myself to relating the episode.

Monsieur Heidenreich lived at 88 boulevard Beaumarchais in an apartment on the same floor as the actor Adolphe Laferrière.[13] My colleague met Monsieur Heidenreich while visiting Monsieur Laferrière. He chatted a while with Monsieur de Paris (as Chief Executioners came to be known), who seemed quite friendly indeed. Laferrière invited my colleague to his apartment where he proceeded to relate a series of very strange and gruesome anecdotes.

"Now I'm speaking to a friend, not a journalist, you understand," Heidenreich told him. "So it's understood that you will not breathe a word of our conversation as long as I'm alive."

The journalist promised solemnly to comply with his wishes. But the following day he published a sensational article relating the conversation in minute detail, a decision for which he would soon pay. Two days later, as he was climbing the stairs leading to Laferrière's apartment, a hand of steel seized him by the neck and lifted him off the floor. A fearsome voice droned into his ear, "On your knees, you miserable wretch! On your knees and ask for forgiveness!"

---

[13] An actor known for his roles in romantic dramas, Laferrière (1806-1877) was also a playwright and author of a book of memoirs. He was very popular in England and would later become known as the Dorian Grey of his day, for he hardly seemed to age at all over a period of twenty years.

Fearing for his life, the journalist dropped to his knees and begged forgiveness. Heidenreich, without saying so much as a word, released him and went back to his apartment. The journalist dashed madly down the stairs, took to his bed for a week, and never returned to visit Laferrière.

Monsieur Heidenreich died March 29, 1872, Good Friday. He was seventy years of age and had fifty-four years of service behind him. He had begun at the age of sixteen alongside his father who was the executioner at the penal facility in Toulon.[14]

At Monsieur Heidenreich's death, his first adjunct, Nicholas Roch, was appointed to replace him as "Chief Executioner for the entire continent of France."[15] Roch's appointment dates from April 6, 1872. It provided an annual salary of six thousand francs to be disbursed monthly. It required him to reside in Paris and to seek written permission should he wish to leave the city for any reason. He was assigned five adjunct executioners to assist him in carrying out his charge as the need arose.

I shall refrain from tracing a complete portrait of Monsieur Roch at this point. The many accounts that follow will accomplish that task. I shall, however, supply a brief biographical sketch. He was born in Mende in the Department of Lozère the 7th of January 1813. The

---

[14] This text is not without ironies. Both Grison and Guillotin were from Saintes. Heidenreich and his father served at the Bagne de Toulon, the penal facility where Hugo's Jean Valjean was incarcerated and where Javert worked as adjutant guard.

[15] At this point Grison elects to reproduce Roch's appointment documents. In the interest of readability, the information contained therein is presented in narrative form.

son of a family of executioners dating back to his great-grandfather, his early years differed little from those of other boys his age. He attended a local primary school where, it must be said, he did not distinguish himself in any way. Soon, his father began grooming him to be his successor. Thus, at the age of ten, he was already accompanying his father as he carried out his duties. When he received his initial appointment in 1831, he had already accumulated several years of experience.

In 1833, in the month of September, François Roch, executioner for the Department of Lozère, was assigned, along with his son Nicholas, to travel to Peirebeilhe to assist his uncle Pierre Roch, Executioner of the Department of Ardèche, in carrying out a triple execution. The condemned were, Martin (called Leblanc) and Marie Breysse (his wife) and Rochette (nicknamed Fétiche), the terrible innkeepers of Peirebeilhe who had finally been called to task after twenty-six years of crime and murder.

It was there that young Nicholas Roch, as he watched the scaffold being erected, posed quite matter-of-factly a telling question: "How do you decide to which side you make the head fall?"

His uncle, taken aback by the young man's nonchalance, hesitated a moment before responding, "Why, in the direction of the prisoner's dwelling."

"Ah, just as we do," Nicholas replied, "and rightly so. It's only fitting."

It is easy to see that already he was primed for the job.

Sometime later Nicholas Roch was named adjunct executioner at Carpentras in the Vaucluse Department where he remained a mere six months because the position was eliminated. He then went back to Mende to assist his father. In 1838 he returned again to Carpentras to accept the appointment of temporary adjunct executioner, replacing Monsieur Oswald Carré (who had been relieved of his duties for refusing to oversee the execution of Jean-Louis Chabert).[16]

In 1843, he assumed the position of adjunct executioner at Lons-le-Saulnier in the Jura Department at a salary of 800 francs, as a replacement for François Demoret, who had been terminated owing to drunkenness. In 1848 he was promoted and his salary increased to 1,200 francs. During his ten-year tenure at Lons-le-Saulnier, he oversaw only one execution but was called on twenty-three times to assist colleagues in neighboring departments.

It was in that capacity in 1851 that he participated in the execution of the poacher Claude Montcharmont at Chalon-sur-Saône (Saône et Loire Department). It was a tumultuous event that attracted a great deal of attention, especially because of an article published in *L'Événement* by Charles Hugo[17] who took the executioners to task and reproached Roch for having quarreled with the executioner in charge.

Montcharmont had been sentenced the 7th of November of 1850 for having murdered two gendarmes and a rural policeman. The 10th of May 1851, the scaffold was erected on the Place Ronde in Chalon. But when

---

[16] *Palmarès 1832-1870* lists no reference to the execution of Jean-Louis Chabert. See "Les Têtes qui tombent," at *guillotine.voila.net1832-1870*.

[17] Victor Hugo's second son (1826-1871). See Chapter Thirty-Four for Victor's role in the matter and consequences for journalists.

officials came for the prisoner, he had barricaded himself in his cell. After a lengthy struggle, he was bound loosely hand and foot and led to a tumbril to be transported to the scaffold.

Having been removed from the tumbril, he was being guided up the stairs to the platform on which the guillotine was erected when he managed to hook his legs around the wooden steps and, with all the strength that his muscular arms and broad shoulders could generate, held on tight. Try as they might, the two local executioners, one of advanced age and the other quite frail, failed utterly to dislodge him. There ensued a terrible struggle. Montcharmont, whose strength and determination were bolstered by the bleak event that awaited him, remained there, doubled up, his eyes fixed with intent, his arms and legs glued unmovably to the structure. He screamed for someone to come to his aid. He called out to his mother and father.

After a good half hour of futile endeavor, efforts were terminated and the prisoner was returned to his cell where he continued to scream. The guillotine remained in place the entire day, surrounded by the crowd. Finally, at four: thirty in the afternoon, the executioner from Dijon arrived, having been called in by the solicitor general. Montcharmont was bound again, but this time in such a way that he could not move at all. Gendarmes and soldiers together cleared the square, and the law prevailed.

Monsieur Roch recounted the dramatic events from his particular point of view. "It was the egotism of my colleague from Chalon," he insisted, "that was the source of the problem. I wanted to bind the prisoner quite fast, a method that had never failed me and would not have failed me today. The proof of the matter became evident when the executioner from Dijon arrived. The bindings in place, his presence was no longer necessary. What I wanted to do in the morning was accomplished in the evening and all went delightfully well."

The 21st of March, 1853, Monsieur Roch was appointed chief executioner at Amiens in the Somme Department. He replaced Henry Ganié, whose charge was revoked for drunkenness, for neglecting to carry out assigned duties, for failure to arrive at the prescribed time for the execution of Madame Gain, and for his refusal to ride in the vehicle with the condemned woman.[18]

During his lengthy tenure at Amiens, Roch participated in numerous executions. "I haven't kept track," he told me later, "but I think the number must be nearly thirty." The log he kept until his Paris appointment, and which I have been able to consult, allows us to establish a more accurate accounting of the number of heads that fell. It lists the following:

As an assistant, under the auspices of his father, François Roch, he assisted at twenty-seven (27) executions; at Lons-le-Saulnier, he oversaw one (1) and assisted at twenty-three (23), and at Amiens thirty (30), for a total of eight-one (81). Under the auspices of Monsieur Heidenreich he assisted at ten (10) executions, for a combined total of ninety-one (91).

As Chief Executioner of the French Continent, he oversaw eighty-two (82) executions, for a grand total of one hundred seventy-three (173).

Monsieur Roch's final execution as a provincial executioner was that of Clément-Modeste Bellières, which took place the 21st of January 1869 at Beauvais (Oise

---

[18] Marie-Josèphe Bruneau, épouse Gain was executed August 25, 1852 at Laon (Picardy).

Department).[19] Bellières was convicted of parricide. By his own admission, he had twisted a knife in his father's heart "as though it were a pat of butter."

The 24th of July, 1871, Nicholas Roch was named executioner adjunct first class at Paris.

As an aide to Monsieur Heidenreich, as I stated earlier, Roch had participated in ten executions. Here is the list:

1–25 October, 1871, at Chaumont: name unknown[20]
2–13 December [November], 1871, at Le Mans (Sarthe): Férier [Perrier], René
3–30 January, 1872 at Saint-Bonnet (Chantal): Ondé, Antoine

---

[19] *Palmarès 1832-1870* (*http//guillotine.voila.net1832-1870*) lists the date as January 21, 1870, the crime having been committed in October of 1869.

[20] *Palmarès des executions de 1871 à 1977* lists the sole execution in Chaumont in 1871 as taking place on the 28th of August, the condemned bearing the name Michel-August Bourgund. The execution was overseen by Heidenreich, but Roch's name is not mentioned (*http//guillotine.voila.net1871-1977*). Grison, as he states, was working with Roch's personal log. Additions and discrepancies have been drawn from the above online public sources: omitted first names have been added; other differing information has been enclosed in brackets; parentheses indicate the department where the execution took place, a nickname, or an alias. At first glance, it may seem unnecessary to reproduce this lengthy catalog of executions. It does have the virtue of humanizing the process to some degree; it also documents the numerous locations involved and the extensive travel required.

4,5,6–19 February, 1872, at Chartres (Eure et Loire): Guénard, Louis; Quillou, Eugène; Proust, Jean-François

7, 8–27 February, 1872, at Saint-Michel (Meuse): Lagagne [Lahaye], Armand; Gerbaud [Gerbeaux], Catherine

9–5 March, 1872, at Marquise (Pas-de-Calais): Lemettre, François-Joseph

10–11 March, 1872, at Versailles: Brunet [Brûlé], Gustave

Hereafter follows the list of the eighty-two executions overseen by Monsieur Roch as Chief Executioner:

1–4 April, 1872, at Troyes: Bourgogne, Léon-Constant

2–8 April [9 April], 1872 at Melun: Ducorbier , Auguste-Isaïe

3, 4–17 April [13 April], 1872, at Charleville (Ardennes): Loth, Jean-Baptiste-Auguste; Lombin, Félicité, épouse Loth

5–19 April, 1872, at Dijon: Rouette, Pierre-Jean

6–29 April [22 April], 1872, at Aix-en-Provence: Tourres, Joseph

7–17 June, 1872, at Paris: Moreux, Jean-Baptiste

8–6 July, 1872, at Caen: Mancel, Charles-Manuel ("Jean")

9–27 July, 1872, at Toulouse: Beltrau [Beltran-Trem, Francisco]

10, 11–29 July, 1872, at Marseille: Sibon, Isaac; Toledano, Raphaël

12–31 July, 1872, at Lyon: Bernard, Batthéléy

13–3 August, 1872, at Arras: Courcol, Jean-Baptiste Joseph

14–16 August, 1872, at Amiens: Gauché [Cauchy, Théophile Hyacinthe]

15, 16–October 1, 1872, at Aix-en-Provence: Gabarino, Luigi ("Le Bachin"); Galetto, Antonio ("Le Bochou")
17–6 January, 1873, at Besançon: Piéglin, Jean-Pierre
18–10 January, 1873, at Reims: Garel, Pierre-Auguste
19–14 January, 1873, at Rennes: Marchand [Lemarchand, Christian-Ernest]
20, 21–14 February, 1873, at Lyon: Vulliard, Jean-Louis; Perré [Perret], Claude
22–25 March, 1873, at Laon: Gard [Guyard, Augustin]
23–29 March, 1873, at Riom: Hébrard, François-Jacques
24–9 April, 1873, at Melun: Sévin, Jean Napoléon
25–15 April, 1873, at Angers: Gautier, François-Adrien ("Isidore")
26–19 April, 1873, at Nantes: Yturmendi, Ignatio
27–24 April, 1873, at Lyon: Vachot, Antoine
28–24 May, 1873, at Paris: Couturier, Antoine
29–27 May, 1873, at Châlon-sur-Saône: Rissé [Rissler, Philippe]
30–26 July, 1873, at Laon: François [Ferrari], Jean-Baptiste
31–14 October [11 October], 1873, at Châteaudun (Eure-et-Loire): Hulans, Jean-Pierre
32–15 October, 1873, at Carcassonne: Praval [Pradal, Antonin]
33–11 December, 1873, at Varennes-sur-Allier (Allier): Rondepierre, Blaise
34–15 January, 1874, at Tulle (Corrèze): Torrisin [Torrison], Pierre
35–8 April, 1874, at Bayonne: Gissal, Carillon [Carillo-Gestal, Damian]
36–10 April, 1874, at Poitiers: Marsand [Marsault], Jean
37, 38–21 April, 1874, at Toulouse: Sevaineur, Philippe; Lasserre, Pierre [Le Vaineur, Philippe ("Mitron, Eugène")]

39–30 June, 1874, at Pibrac (Haute-Garonne): Cerisat [Céseriat], Antoine
40–15 September, 1874, at Vesoul (Haute Saône): Poissi [Poisse], Jean-François
41–19 September [28 September], 1784, at Chartres: Poirier, Sylvain-Louis
42–3 October, 1784, at Nîmes: Mariani, Joseph-Marie
43–13 October, 1874, at Paris: Moreau, Pierre-Désiré; Boudas, Charles[21]
44–20 October, 1874, at Châlon-sur-Saône: Gaulfat [Goulfert], André
45–14 December, 1874, at Moulins (Allier): Caillot, Joseph-Hippolyte
46–2 February, 1875, at Nîmes: Terrier, François
47–31 March, 1875, at Paris: Bacquet, Pierre-Louis
48–15 April, 1875, at Cambrai (Nord): Ruffin, Léon-Pierre
49–22 June, 1875, at Épinal (Vosges): Labauvoye [Labanvoye], Nicholas
50–10 July, 1875, at Beaucaire (Gard): Sanchon, François [Sancho y Carreta, Francisco]
51–13 July, 1875, at Toulouse: Rieubernt, François ("Besse,") [("Abadie")]
52–2 August, 1875, at Bordeaux: Fradon, Jean
53–15 November, 1875, at Nancy: Chaussy, François
54–9 December, 1875, at Draguignan (Var): Allongue, Jean-Honoré
55–31 December, 1875, at Nancy: Gervais [Greveis], Jean-Baptiste ("Émile")
56–4 January, 1876, at Bourg [Le Bourg] (Lot): Gontier [Gautié], Sophie, épouse Bouyon, veuve Colombe

---

[21] Grison's numbering does not reflect the double execution, as it does elsewhere.

57–8 January, 1876, at Rennes: Riaud, Joseph
58–15 June, 1876, at Valence (Drôme): Courbis, André
59–3 July, 1876, at Bordeaux: Pascal, Jean-Baptiste
60–12 August, 1876, at Paris: Gervais, Toussaint-Léon
61–2 September, 1876, at Perpignan: Segundo, Roldin Moralès
62–18 September, 1876, at Blois: Marin, Maxime
63–14 December, 1876, at Nice: Turcan, Marius
64–20 [23] December, 1876, at Douai (Nord): Yden, Louis-Charles [Charles-Louis]
65–27 December, 1876, at Toulouse: Ducaux, Julien
66–24 March, 1877, at Saint-Mihiel (Meuse): Moulut, Charles-Émile
67–25 [26] April, 1877, at Paris, Billoir, Baptiste-Joseph
68–12 May, 1877, at Tarbes (Hautes-Pyrénées): Badel, François
69–21 June, 1877, at Versailles: Roux, Ange-Valentin
70–22 [23] June, 1877, at Angers: Changeur, Augustin [Auguste]
71, 72–28 June, 1877, at Douai (Nord): Aublin, Léonard-Théophile; Hubet, Julien [Hubet is not listed]
73–17 August, 1877, at Marseille: Vitalis, Léon-Paul
74–11 September, 1877, at Paris: Welker, Jean-Pierre
75–13 September, 1877, at Laon (Aisne): Clovis [Frison], Jean-Sylvestre
76–25 October, 1877, at Paris: Albert, Antoine-Joseph
77–4 [5] January, 1878, at Melun (Seine-et-Marne): Corsinesco, Louis-Théophile [Luigi Teofilo]
78–22 February, 1878, at Aix-en-Provence: Siméan, Jean-Marie
79–18 March, 1878, at Evreux (Eure): Louchard, Emanuel-Modeste
80–13 July, 1878, at Lyon: Laurent, Jean-Pierre

81, 82–7 September, 1878, at Paris: Barr, Aimé; Lebiez, Paul

In reality this fearsome public employee was the finest man imaginable. He was married and the father of eight children, four boys and four girls. His eldest daughter married Monsieur Berger, one of her father's assistants.

His widow continues to live at the same address where her husband died, 8 rue Rochebrune (formerly rue Nouvel), on the third floor. She cherished her husband and has retained a cult-like memory of him. Nothing pleases her more than to hear someone praise his performance as Chief Executioner. "Ah, yes," she is fond of saying, "you might find another who will do as well, but no one could do better."

Her daughter, Madame Berger, is a beautiful, young, blond woman who speaks thoughtfully of her father's indescribable kindness. He loved to play with young children, she says, as though he were a child himself.

One peculiarity: when he was assigned to the provinces, he always wore two gold earrings of which he appeared particularly fond. Once he was named Chief Executioner in Paris, however, he felt compelled to give them up.

Nicholas Roch died of apoplexy the 21st of April, 1879. He was succeeded by one of his aides, Louis-Antoine Deibler, about whom I shall have more to say later.

CHAPTER THREE
An Accounting of the Executions

I have just a few words to say before finishing with preliminaries and beginning my eyewitness accounts of the executions I have attended. At this point I would like to draw the readers' attention to the statistics relative to the number of death sentences rendered in France and the number of executions actually carried out since the beginning of the century.

From 1800 to 1825, that is to say the first quarter of the century, 6,665 death sentences were rendered, out of which, despite the absence of official statistics, one can deduct more than half owing to appeals and commutations. The remaining three thousand translate as an average of one hundred twenty executions per year.

For this period, the largest number of condemnations rendered occurred in 1816 (514), 1817(558), and 1818 (321); whereas the smallest number of condemnations rendered occurred in 1811 (183), 1824 (201), and 1825 (176).

From 1825 to 1850 the number of death sentences decreased significantly. During this period only 1,563 such sentences were rendered, out of which 999 were actually carried out, that is to say, some 40 per year. It is true that certain modifications in the penal code were brought to bear. The penalty for forgery of bank notes, for example, was reduced to forced labor, and, if mitigating circumstances could be proved, the penalty for arson was almost never imposed. Moreover, the number of death sentences in only the first three years exceeded one hundred: 1826 (150), 1827 (109), and 1828 (114). Certain other years counted very low condemnations: 1831 (25), 1836 (30), and 1837 (33). The proportion of executions for the period runs approximately 75%, except for 1840, when out of 51 condemnations, only 6 commutations were accorded.

From 1850 to 1860 the figures continue to decline. For the decade 283 executions resulted from 502 condemnations: that is to say, some 50 condemnations and 28 executions per year. The highest figures are recorded for 1851 (79 condemnations/37 executions) and 1855 (61 condemnations/28 executions). The lowest figures are recorded for the years 1858, 1859, and 1860: 39 condemnations for each of the three years with two-thirds resulting in executions.

The declining numbers continue for the years 1860 to 1870: a mere 193 condemnations, out of which 84 were commuted. Out of the average of 11 executions per year, the years 1864, 1866, and 1870 stand out. In each of these years the dreaded blade fell only five times!

After the (Franco-Prussian) war, the number of condemnations continued to fall, but the percentage of executions began to rise. In 1871, out of 16 condemnations, ten executions took place. In 1872, there were 31 condemnations and 21 executions. In 1873, there were 31 condemnations and 15 executions. In 1874, there were 31 condemnations and 12 executions. In 1875, there were 33 condemnations and 10 executions. And for 1876, there were 22 condemnations and 10 executions. For the years 1877 to 1883, the number of condemnations more or less maintains pace with perhaps a slight rise, despite the clemency–some say weakness–of juries, but the number of executions decreases.

The rise in condemnations, however slight, is perhaps due to the reluctance of juries to impose the death sentence. Criminals reason that since there is a good chance a death sentence will be commuted, they no longer fear the law to the same degree. Therefore the number of murders is on the rise.

It's all too logical.

And now I shall begin my eye-witness accounts with the first execution Monsieur Roch, as Chief Executioner of the French Continent, oversaw in Paris, assisted by five adjuncts, Messieurs Gagne, Desfourneaux, Berger, Deibler, and Étienne.

CHAPTER FOUR
The Execution of Jean-Baptiste Moreux
(Paris, 17 June 1872)

Jean-Baptiste Moreux has left scarcely a trace in the annals of crime. He was a run-of-the-mill criminal whose sentencing was hardly noticed amidst the attention received by other trials ongoing in the city. He was a herculean figure who robbed and murdered a prostitute in order to provide for his wife. It is even said that when she was called to appear at criminal court, she was wearing one of the victim's dresses. I cannot confirm it was so, but what is certain is this: Moreux had indeed given the victim's clothes to his wife, saying that he had bought them in the Temple Quarter. When arrested he did not deny having committed the crime. He was sentenced to death the 13th of May, 1872; and on the 17th of June he was executed.

In truth, the public had become quite blasé with regard to courtroom histrionics and executions. Few people mulled about the Place de la Roquette. Some twenty night owls, who had heard about the execution after supper, and a few journalists, their notebooks in hand, constituted the meager audience that would see the final act of this drama play out.

And yet there were two aspects that were out of the ordinary. The guillotine had not been used in Paris for ten years, and Monsieur Heidenreich had died. Too, word had it that the mechanism of death had undergone complete modification. As the guard at the condemned prisoners ward naïvely put it, "The scaffold is no more. All that remains is the guillotine."

The curiosity seekers were responding to the dual enticement of a new apparatus and a new executioner. They watched with great interest as the guillotine was assembled. It is well known that five stone slabs, placed in front of the prison gate, served as supports for the structure. They are what local thieves term in their colorful jargon "Saint Peter's Abbey." During his imprisonment, the outlaw poet François-Pierre Lacenaire[22] dedicated to them the following lines of poetry:

> *Oh! je vous connais bien, dalles qui faites place*
> *Aux quatre pieds de l'échafaud,*
> *Dalles de pierre blanche où ne reste plus trace*
> *Du sang versé par le bourreau.*

> Oh! I know you well, slabs that provide a footing
> For the four legs of the scaffold,
> Slabs of white stone where remains nary a trace
> Of the blood spilt by the executioner.

In the new configuration, only the central slab is utilized. Two pieces of wood are placed on top of the slab. It is upon them that the two uprights rest, each of

---

[22] Lacenaire (born in 1803 in Lyon), a poet and murderer, may be viewed as France's O. Henry. Writing poetry in his cell, he garnered quite a public following. His story attracted the attention of writers such as Théophile Gautier (who devoted a section of the poem "Étude de mains" to him), Balzac, and Dostoyevsky. He is the subject of the film *Les enfants du paradis* (*The Children of Paradise*), directed by Marcel Carné, screenplay by Jacques Prévert. He was executed in 1836.

them five meters in height and fitted on their inner side with grooves to allow for the sliding of the mouton (the heavy weight), as well as the blade and the upper portion of the lunette or collar. In front of it a rather large metal receptacle resembling a large coal bucket is placed to receive the head and designed to prevent it from rolling about hideously. Behind, a wicker basket lined with sheet metal and full of sawdust is place to the right of the bascule. A vertical plank is located at the end of the structure. Another smaller plank placed obliquely leads down to the basket. It is on it that the body will slide after the execution.

The wood is painted in a dark color. The blade is no longer shiny as it used to be. At ten paces, all one can see are the two uprights and the heavy, cast iron mouton that provides the force to propel it at an ever-increasing speed in its descent.

One of the assistants has described it as "a large sewing machine."

On that day the spectators expected to see the mechanism tested on a bail of straw, according to custom. But they were disappointed. The executioner simply slid the mouton up and down in its grooves until he was satisfied that the system was functioning properly.

Monsieur Roch was watched closely by the crowd as he made his debut. He was the new executioner and, after all, he was from the provinces.

People had come with the expectation of seeing a strange looking, savage, gigantesque fellow. What they saw was a man with a placid and calm countenance, dressed in a stylish frock coat of quality, his hair well brushed, and wearing brand new, kid leather boots with patent leather toes. From his paunchy abdomen hung an oversized gold chain. His graying whiskers, his hooked nose, and his small, gray, eyes did not seem at all unusual. It was a face that people see every day.

Monsieur Roch might well have been taken for a well-to-do, retired carpenter or a country bailiff dressed in Sunday attire. In the darkness he went about his business; he inspected with fatherly care the installation of the apparatus, had a wedge placed here, tightened a screw there, cleaned the rust from a spring, or wiped away the moisture of an early-morning mist. His lantern in hand, when at last he had determined that everything was in order, he pulled out a cigar, carefully removed the end with a penknife, lit it, returned the knife and box of matches to his pocket, and produced billows of smoke with the satisfaction of a proud bourgeois exalting in the tidiness of his kitchen.

He showed no emotion. He maintained this tranquil demeanor unless a serious development interceded, an accident or a major glitch. After all, he was virtually born into the profession. As a very young boy in Amiens, he assisted his father at the exhibitions of the stocks that took place on market days. Later, he became his father's second assistant and was soon charged with the duties of first assistant. Thus, before replacing Monsieur Heidenreich in Paris, he had already participated in many executions.

At about four o'clock in the morning, a small group of people could be seen surrounding him. He was asked several questions. He answered them straightforwardly. He was not bothered because he didn't know anyone in the group. When he was asked by a police officer whether he had assisted Monsieur Heidenreich at Jean-Baptiste Troppmann's execution, he replied modestly: "No, I wasn't a party to that affair."

The execution was scheduled for five o'clock. At four: twenty, Father Crozes, the venerable condemned prisoners' chaplain, arrived. Just as the priest was entering the prison followed by Monsieur Claude, head of security, and by Monsieur Isembert, the appeals clerk, some smart aleck kid in the crowd bellowed out Hervé's famous refrain:[23]

*On va lui couper la tête,
C'est bien fait!*

His head is going to fall,
Once and for all!

These lines taken from *l'Oeil crevé* (*The Blind Eye*) might be quite funny in a performance at the Folies-Dramatiques,[24] but at this place and time they made shivers run up and down people's spines. They made a person want to strangle the kid.

I talked with an elderly guard about what the condemned prisoner had been doing.

"He knows what's happening," he said. "For the past hour he has been pacing back and forth in his cell and smoking his pipe."

"Is he overwhelmed or resigned?" I asked.

"Well, he'll be quite composed."

The elderly guard was spot on. When Father Crozes told Moreux that the hour of atonement was neigh, the prisoner received the fatal news quite calmly.

---

[23] Florimond Rongé, known as Hervé (1825-1892), composer of widely popular, often pernicious, operettas.

[24] Paris theater reputed for staging operettas, those of Jacques Offenbach, for example.

"Oh, I thought it wouldn't be until Wednesday," is all he said.

He then put down his pipe and confessed his sins and asked for penitence. The court clerk read his sentence and notified him of the rejection of his appeal. He was then accompanied to the registry. His hair being worn rather short, little time was required for his grooming.

Monsieur Roch arrived to apply the bindings.

"Isn't there some way we can dispense with that," the prisoner asked.

"That's impossible."

"Well then, go ahead, Monsieur."

A rope was loosely tied around his ankles and his hands were tied behind his back. He refused the glass of water offered him, and despite his bindings, he moved forward at an assured pace.

The prison's arched iron gate swung open. The prisoner appeared accompanied by the five aides and the executioner, all dressed in black and looking like undertakers.

Half way to the scaffold Father Crozes stopped and kissed the prisoner.[25] He then gave him a crucifix to kiss and scurried to his vehicle. Moreux turned his head in the priest's direction and said upon seeing the head guard on his left, "Adieu, Morel. You see where vice leads."

The prisoner turned his head again and saw the glint of the blade, his eyes suddenly wild and blinking. He lowered his head and walked quickly toward the bascule.

---

[25] The holy kiss originated in early Christendom. It was integrated into the Catholic liturgy as the kiss of peace. It was as such that it found its way into execution solemnities.

Three thuds were heard. The body rolled into one basket and the head into the other.

The execution was over.

Just as the aide in the front began lifting the head and wiping away the blood from its beard so that it could be reunited with the body in the hearse, two loud whistles were heard. They come from those in the crowd who felt that the spectacle was over far too soon.

CHAPTER FIVE
*The Execution of Antoine Couturier
(Paris, 24 May 1873)*

"It was her fault, too. Why did she defy me?"

That was the sole justification Antoine Couturier offered the jury when he was accused of murdering his wife.

Couturier was sixty years old. He was a tall, handsome man who wore a short, stiff, white mustache that made him look like a former military man. But the army had not been his profession. The only uniform he had worn was the black attire and shiny hat of an undertaker.

Having left that profession, Couturier became a wine merchant on the boulevard de Vaugirard. And a strange wine merchant he was, for he believed he could increase sales by drinking all day. His wife, who saw their household declining, quarreled with him incessantly until one day he threw down his apron and declared that henceforth he would do nothing at all.

Better still, he went out and rented a room for himself. Yet if he no longer appeared behind the counter, that did not prevent him from becoming an all-too-regular customer, and an undesirable customer at that– because he had the habit of drinking a lot and never paying.

Of course his wife did not interpret his retirement from business in that fashion. So she continued to express her anger.

The eleventh of December, 1872, at seven o'clock in the morning, he returned home, as was his habit, to begin drinking again. His wife, seeing that he was already tipsy, told him there was no wine to be had.

"I don't believe you," Couturier said as he grabbed a jug. "I'll just go to the cellar and see for myself."

"I won't allow it!" his wife shouted.

"It's not the likes of you who will prevent me from doing as I please."

"Oh, really? I'm going to lock the cellar door."

"You'd better not. If you go down to the cellar, you'll regret it."

" Just try it, you no good . . . !"

"Don't defy me!"

"That's exactly what I'm doing."

So Couturier went down the cellar, followed closely by his wife who threatened him at every step. At the bottom of the stairs, he picked up an axe that was lying next to a pile of wood and waved it in her face.

"Don't tell me '*no*,' or you've had it."

"*No, no, no*, you big coward!" his wife cried out.

With one blow of the axe, Couturier split his wife's skull all the way to her shoulders. Not satisfied, he gave her two more whacks. Then, as calmly as you please, he filled his jug and went about his drinking.

During the day, when people began asking after his wife, without a second thought he related the morning's drama. Having been arrested, he told the story first to the police and then to the investigating magistrate. Before the jury, he repeated it complacently, using his favorite expression:

"It was her fault. She shouldn't have defied me."

"Why did you strike her three times," asked the foreman of the jury, "when, by your own admission, she was dead after the first blow?"

"It was well and truly to be done with her," the accused replied with satisfaction.

The jury found him guilty without mitigating circumstances. Yet, considering him to be mentally irresponsible, the jurors all signed an appeal for mercy.

The appeal was denied, and the execution was carried out the 24th of May.

The Police department was very strict about admitting individuals to the enclosed area. The sole means possible was written authorization signed by the Ministry of Justice. Therefore there were few people around the scaffold.

At four o'clock in the morning Couturier was still sleeping. He was awakened by Father Crozes. The sight of the priest at that hour made the prisoner quite aware of the reason for his presence.

Keeping his cool, he asked, "So it's really true? That's funny, because I was hoping my appeal would be granted."

"You need to resign yourself my son . . ."

"It was quite useless to make me wait so long. But it's hard, nevertheless."

The appeals clerk, Monsieur Aussilloux, the superintendent of the prison police, Monsieur Claude, the head of security, and the warden all tried to reassure him. Couturier brushed them off brashly.

"I'll take it like a man," he said. "I'm not the kind to quake in my boots."

"Would you like to write a note for your family?" Monsieur Claude inquired.

"Don't bother!"

"Would you like something to eat or drink?" the warden asked.

"What good would that do? I'm going to die."

"When Monsieur Roch came in, Couturier couldn't help reacting."

"Do you know who this man is?" Monsieur Claude asked.

"I certainly do!"

The prisoner's preparations began. Feeling the cold scissors against his neck, he shivered and asked for some brandy. Two small glasses were brought in. He downed them the one after the other.

"Is it going all right?" he asked Monsieur Roch.

His restraints being in place, the registration procedure was completed. At five minutes after five the large double gate of the Roquette prison swung open.

Couturier appeared to lean on two aides. Before him, Father Crozes walked backwards, facing him, seeking to block his view of the guillotine. But because the good priest is short of stature, the prisoner was able to see over his head and glimpse the blade.

In so doing, he gave such a start that the two men were nearly knocked down. Then, regaining his composure he walked unsteadily toward the guillotine. No sooner had he kissed the crucifix when the aides pushed him down violently and prodded his neck under the lunette.

At that moment the prisoner recoiled mightily. The aide holding his head immediately forced it down again. Legend has it that Couturier was guillotined twice, the first attempt cutting of no more than his chin, making it necessary to raise the blade again to finish the job.

I was present at the execution and viewed the cadaver an hour later at the Gentilly cemetery. I can tell you exactly how that legend came to be.

When Couturier recoiled, the aide had to force his head back into position again. The result was that his chin was slammed against the copper edging of the lunette. The concussion caused blood to spurt. Also, because the aide's hand was momentarily between the two grooves, the release mechanism could not be activated immediately. There was therefore an interval of a few seconds between securing the prisoner on the bascule and the release of the blade.

Such is the origin of the legend of Antoine Couturier, the man who was guillotined twice.

CHAPTER SIX
The Charbonnières Crime Spree
(The Manhunt)

People today still recall the mysterious string of murders that took place in Digny and Charbonnières and which, coupled with the murders committed in Limours, spread terror throughout the region.[26] The public and authorities alike believed the same person or persons to be responsible for the murderous acts. The crimes were all so similar, the same modus operandi as at Limours, the same as at Forges and at Vaugrigneuses. As for the Digny and Charbonnières crimes, police believed the perpetrator to be someone from the region, a carpenter, cabinetmaker, woodsman, or an individual of that ilk.

The authorities of Nogent-le-Rotrou went to unbelievable lengths to discover the identity of the criminal(s).[27] Extensive searches had been ordered by the investigating magistrate, Monsieur Allaire, who had personally assumed the direction of the gendarmerie. Unfortunately, the countryside is traversed by forest, hedges, and dense brush. Houses are quite isolated, making crime easier there than elsewhere and making such

---

[26] Grison's note: Five murders had been committed successively in the region of Chartres. Each victim had been struck down at night, at home, without the murderer leaving a clue. The police suspected an organized gang. The terror did not subside until the Bazoche case finally brought the perpetrator to justice.

[27] Nogent-le-Rotrou lies some fifty miles west of Chartres.

searches all the more difficult. (I myself came to that conclusion during my stay there.)

Hope of finding the murderers was rapidly fading when, the 25th of May, 1874, another crime was committed near the village of Bazoche-Gouet.

Monsieur and Madame Travers left their farm after the midday meal and traveled to Charbonnières to attend the fair. They had left their two children behind to guard the farm. They returned early so that their children could take a turn at the fair themselves. Upon arriving home, a horrible scene awaited them. Their son and their daughter lay on the ground in a pool of blood. The daughter was dead. The son was still alive but was in a horrible state. A chunk of his skull had been chopped out by an axe.

Robbery had been the motive of the crime. Between five and six hundred francs were missing. Monsieur de Marolles, the public prosecutor, and Monsieur Allaire rushed to the crime scene in order to begin the investigation. The investigation lasted several days, at the conclusion of which strong suspicion fell upon a sawyer named Sylvain-Louis Poirier who lived nearby.

The 25th of May, the day of the crime, the parents had not told anyone outside their household of their plans to attend the fair. The murderer must have encountered them on their way to Charbonnières. What is more, familiarity with the farmhouse, where to find the keys, and several other details led to the conclusion that the criminal knew his way around the place and therefore was someone local.

Now Poirier lived at a place called la Bahine that is located along the route Monsieur and Madame Travers followed to the fair. He had also worked on their farm on several occasions. Yet, for all that, he seemed a most unlikely suspect to people living in the area.

However, magistrates recalled a report of a suspicious character observed in the vicinity of Charbonnières on the day of another crime committed in the area. That report contained a rather accurate description of an individual resembling Poirier. A warrant was obtained and his house was searched. Poirier himself was nowhere to be found. The search uncovered a shotgun and a pistol, but nothing of a suspicious nature. His wife, however, was not able to confirm his whereabouts on the day of the crime.

An arrest warrant was issued. Three gendarmes were stationed along the road at the edge of the village. During this time Poirier had made his way to Châteaudun and had gone to an inn where he sat around with some of his friends discussing police efforts relating to the case. Along with his friends he vilified the perpetrators and called for them to be brought to justice.

All of a sudden two gendarmes reined in their horses in front of the inn after having completed an inspection tour. Upon seeing them, Poirier quickly slipped out the back door and disappeared so stealthily that his comrades did not know he had left. After a moment they called out after him. The gendarmes realized what had happened and ran after him, to no avail.

Messieurs de Marolles and Allaire immediately issued a call for a force of men to track him down. Eight hundred peasants from surrounding villages answered the call and armed themselves with an array of weapons: aging firearms, pitchforks, scythes, and iron rods. They were divided into small groups headed by a gendarme, and the search began.

The force was divided into two main contingents. Each of them set out in opposite directions to enclose in an immense circle eight kilometers in diameter the area where Poirier was thought to be hiding. When the two contingents met to complete the circle, the men all began to move toward the center, forming an ever-shrinking ring of men.

Before long, Poirier was seen bounding out of a thicket attempting to get away. He was confronted by twenty men brandishing guns or pitchforks. He backtracked and took off in another direction, only to encounter the same impasse.

At this point, I am going to turn over the account to an eyewitness who related it to me on the very site where Poirier was flushed out, at Étang des Carrières, one of the most picturesque settings in the Montmirail forest.

"He was in the undergrowth," the peasant said, "his head just above the brush, keeping an eye and ear out for the pursuers that were closing in and hoping that they wouldn't see him and would pass him by.

"Several peasants suddenly appeared in the nearby clearing. Poirier ducked down and began to move away, but not in time. A man from Chapelle-Guillaume got a glimpse of him and fired a shot into the air forewarning the others.

"Poirier bounded out of the undergrowth and disappeared. The men ran after him. Before long he came to the edge of the forest and leaped out into the open.

"Of course he was now in plain view. Twenty shots were fired as a signal. He thought the men were firing at him. He backtracked suddenly, hoping to make it back to the forest where he could hide in the foliage or at least run from tree to tree. He had to try!

"Once again it was too late. The trackers who had first located him ran over to bar his route. So he turned and rushed headlong into a rye field, followed by the shouts of men and the deafening sounds of gunshots on all sides. But he disappeared again. The men had seen the tall stalks part, and then nothing.

"He hadn't escaped from the rye field, however. The men began to search it furrow by furrow," the peasant told me. "Only a faint trail here and there remained. The men would not give up the chase, even if it meant cutting down every stalk in the field. Now a young man from Bazoche-Gouet came upon the murderer in that part of the field there. He was stretched out on his stomach and gasping for breath from his efforts.

"The young peasant lifted his iron pitchfork and shouted, 'Give up, now!'

"But the murderer was not as exhausted as he appeared. Before he could be collared, he leaped to his feet and ran off again at top speed. The peasant set off after him and remained not far behind. It was fantastic to see the two running across the fields, struggling over hedges, leaping ditches filled with water. All that with everyone else following behind, trying desperately to keep up.

"Finally, they came to a low swampy area surrounded by tall thickets. Poirier dove into one of the thickets. The men followed but found nothing. The murderer knew very well how to hide. While the area behind him was being searched, Poirier probably slipped away to the side or doubled back. Those who were in the rear had seen nothing.

"The search party went over the area bush by bush. Nothing!

"We were beginning to feel a bit low when just there," the peasant said, pointing to a small field surrounded by hedges, "we noticed a trail in the grass. None of our party had gone there yet. It suddenly became clear. Poirier had followed the ditch behind the hedge, and we had lost the trail which reappeared only fifty meters down the way. We followed the trail and came upon a dense thicket. One of the men went into the thicket and almost stepped on the murderer who had camouflaged himself in the brush.

"'Let go of me,' Poirier shouted as the man seized him. 'Let go of me, Jacques, or I'll blow your brains out!'

"'Me Jacques, you'll blow my brains out?'

"Other men were coming to help, but, leaping to his feet, the murderer knocked Jacques over and took off again. There were now a large number of men who had been drawn to the area by the gunshots and struggle. They came running from everywhere, from thickets and fields and ditches they surged to surround the fleeing criminal. Poirier zigged and zagged in and out, like a fox that will do anything to make it to his den to hole up. Desperation pushing him to new heights in his effort to escape, he overcame every obstacle. And the men who followed trailed behind, the best of them unable to keep up.

"Nevertheless, the circle was tightening.

"Using the same tactic as before, Poirier ran alongside a hedge and followed it to a pond. The water splashed. He had run into the pond and had disappeared yet again.

"Men gathered around. They looked but saw nothing at first. They began to think Poirier had drowned. But then they noticed a slight movement in the floating vegetation, and upon approaching, they recognized the face they'd been looking for.

"A gendarme grabbed him and dragged him out of the water. Poirier pretended to be unconscious. He was thought to be dead or passed out. The men prepared to help the man. But it was nothing but a ploy. Stretched out on dry land, he realized he was unrestrained and made a vigorous effort to get up and take off again. Twenty arms reached out, pulled him back, and held him down. He struggled, but only a moment before giving up completely."

The crowd was so angry that, without the presence of magistrates and gendarmes, Poirier would have been lynched on the spot. In the end he was escorted by the peasants to the village of Bazoche-Gouet.

An interesting detail. As Poirier was passing by the Travers farm where the murders had taken place, the family dog came running out, leaped viciously upon him, and ended up following the throng for more than a league, howling all the while.

Once in Bazoche, the incredible energy that had fueled Poirier's attempted escape now took another form. Realizing all was lost for him, he was smitten with intermittent fits of great violence. He was able to be interrogated by the magistrates only when an outburst had subsided. Eventually, he confessed having committed the crime.

It was a horrible sight, seeing the miserable wretch foaming at the mouth, writhing in convulsions, and hearing him babble on in a broken voice about his wife, his children, and his fear of burning in hell.

"I'm thirsty, water! water! I'm burning up!" he cried out as he raked his fingernails across his chest. "Oh! I'm so hot, burning hot. I'm in hell. I'm already in hell."

The greatest of precautions were taken when Poirier was transported to Nogent. Such was the animosity of the peasants toward him that the residents of neighboring villages lined the route the entire day waiting for him to pass.

Poirier was a tall man with a low forehead, sunken eyes, and protruding cheekbones, a fierce looking face for sure. He was feared throughout the region.

In prison, for several days he refused to say anything at all when questioned by the judges. As I have stated, after having been tracked down like a wild beast and arrested at the pond in which he was hiding, Poirier had confessed to the murders in a moment of despair. Later, in prison, he tried to deny his confession. Overwhelmed by the evidence, however, he finally owned up and ultimately confessed to the Charbonnières crime as well.

Having ascertained those facts, investigators were not about to stop there. Both the public prosecutor, Monsieur Marolles, and the investigating magistrate reviewed briefs of several other unsolved crimes committed in the surrounding area in the interest of determining what role, if any, Poirier might have played in each one of them.

It goes without saying that in the beginning Poirier vehemently denied involvement in any of them. But, as the evidence mounted and became increasingly incriminating, he became more and more taciturn, more and more worried, to the point that his words began to come out in stuttered babblings, near-admissions he could not prevent from surfacing despite the energy and resolve he had shown up to his capture.

It was only after two weeks of fruitless questioning that interrogators were able to wrench another confession out of him, a confession to another murder. At the end of October, 1871, the Widow Lecomte, at a farm she owned near the village of Gault in the Vendôme, had conducted a sale of her belongings for a considerable sum. She was keeping it on hand until being able to go to town and have it invested by her notary.

On the 1st of November, she was found lying dead next to her elderly maid with whom she lived alone, both of them covered with blood. Both of them had been horribly mutilated with an axe. The axe in question had been taken from a shed on the property. Robbery was the murder's motive. The sideboard in which the sum from the sale was locked had been broken into and the money removed.

Vendôme authorities investigated to no avail. A brother who had mistreated the dead women a few days before was arrested but proved his innocence and was released.

Authorities had all but given up on finding the culprit when certain information came to light following Poirier's arrest. Coincidences led to the suspicion that he may have been involved in the Gault crime. The crimes were so very similar. Poirier was interrogated again. In the face of the determination that he was unable to account for his whereabouts on the day of the Gault crime, he broke down and confessed again.

In the end, the tabulation of Poirier victims would mount to a total of five: the two women near Gault, another area woman named Bézard, and the two Travers children. It was time for justice to take its toll.

Poirier admitted his mistake with unpretentious savagery. He was wrong to do his business so close to home. That, he said, was his undoing.

CHAPTER SEVEN
The Execution of Sylvain-Louis Poirier (29 September 1874)[28]

It was three: thirty in the morning when I arrived in Chartres.

At a spot called Porte Morard, the road ran above a large body of placid water. As though a platinum mirror, its surface, bathed completely in moonlight, reflected perfectly the tall, shimmering poplars, the small, charming houses that might have been out of a comic opera, a mill that awaited daybreak to resume its tic toc, and, farther along, the age-roughened, lacelike gable of a house built in 1350. In the distance, on a dark green hillside dotted with copses, other houses of varying sizes and periods could be seen, interspaced here and there by the silhouettes of small steeples. A poet with any Germanic sensitivity at all would certainly have been moved to see the Wilis passionately dancing above the trees or over the melancholic expanse of water.[29]

At the execution site six carpenters were erecting the guillotine under the direction of Monsieur Roch. Their red lanterns accompanied them as they went about their business. Little by little, at a slow but regular pace, the beheading machine took form amidst some five hundred curious onlookers. Monsieur Roch appeared to be

---

[28] Dating inconsistencies continue into the text itself. Grison originally listed 19 September as the execution date; the public record lists 28 September. See Chapter Two, number 41.

[29] The Wilis are more commonly identified as Slavic.

suffering from a dreadful cold. He urged the workers on in an increasingly hoarse voice. Finally, just before four o'clock, everything appeared ready; the blade, which from a distance resembled a silver triangle, was then tested successfully.

Poirier's execution was scheduled for five: thirty in the morning. While Monsieur Roch saw to final details, I walked to the prison, to which I was assured of gaining access, thanks to the good graces of the deputy public prosecutor, Monsieur de Royer, one of the nicest officials I have ever met.

I was moved to do so because of the opportunity to witness up close the final moments of a condemned man's life–moments that cause a man to age a year a minute. Such opportunities are extremely rare.

I entered the building at three: forty-five. Constructed of stone and brick, it has a rather coquettish appearance; it looks more like a country house than a prison. In the courtyard four dragoons were coming and going. I went into the vestibule where the head guard showed me into the warden's office. When the prosecutor and the priests come in, I thought I'd just follow them and would be able to see everything.

At four: ten a vehicle arrived. Deputy prosecutor de Royer got out; then two priests come in, Father Rousillon (a canon) and Father Durand, nephew of the bishop of Chartres. I heard the sound of horses hooves. It was a brigade from the gendarmerie that had pulled up to the gate. Ten gendarmes headed down the long corridor that runs the length of the prison on the ground floor.

It was time to see to the prisoner. Slowly, the group made its way toward his cell on the next floor. Instinctively, we all removed our hats: we felt part of a funeral procession.

The cell door was open. The cell itself was dimly lighted by a sole, smoking lantern. Poirier was sleeping on his back, a smile on his face. He was a sturdy, muscular man with a stern face, indented forehead, small eyes, and closely cropped blond hair. Everything about him radiated strength. If he decided to resist, the struggle would be intense.

"Poirier," the head guard, Monsieur Prim, said as he shook his shoulder. "Poirier!"

The prisoner blinked his eyes for a moment, sat up, and looked haggardly at the people surrounding him. Suddenly, he shuddered visibly.

"Poirier," Monsieur Prim began again, "your appeal and stay have been rejected. You must have courage. It's for today."

Poirier remained silent for a few seconds. Then, in a strange, monotone voice that did not seem human, he said, "It's okay. It makes no difference to me. I'm only concerned about my poor wife and children."

As he said this, he swung his feet onto the floor. The guards had him put on a pair of old, near-white, ribbed velour trousers and a worker's smock.

"Poirier," Monsieur de Royer asked, "do you have anything you want to tell us? Now, that you are facing God, don't you want to unburden your conscience and tell us whether you had a hand or not in the Limours murders?"

"No," Poirier replied in a stronger voice. "No, no!"

All of us except the two priests left the cell and went back down to the vestibule where the prisoner would undergo final preparations. A quarter of an hour went by in near silence. The only words spoken took the form of a near-whisper. The vestibule was a sinister room. Imagine a high ceiling with bare walls, a floor in red tiles, and low-slung, vaulted doors. It was lighted by a lamp without a shade that was blinding to look at and by four candles. A single ray of moonlight shone through a window and danced on a wooden stool. It was on that stool that the condemned man was to sit.

We heard footsteps. Monsieur Roch and his aides came in. They were all dressed in black frock coats. Monsieur Roch wore a top hat. The others wore Alpine hats. They went into the registry where the executioner signed the prisoner receipt section of the register. Monsieur Roch found that too much time was being taken to deliver the prisoner and it was time to get on with matters. He twirled impatiently the enormous, gold chain that traversed his vest and outlined his stomach.

All of a sudden he walked up to me, brought his hand to the brim of his hat, and said, "Monsieur, does he have the irons on his legs?"

All I could say was that I didn't know.

At five: twenty, the condemned man, who had been in the chapel, came out and asked for something to drink. He was given two measures of tea and rum, which he drained straight away.

Then he was led to that terrible preparation room. He lowered his head and went of his own volition to the stool and sat down. The ray of moonlight that fell upon him now made him appear quite pale. The executioner picked up the shadeless lamp and walked toward him. The light hurt Poirier's eyes. He lifted his head and looked up at Monsieur de Paris, blinking his eyes. He then sat mournfully still.

The executioner and his aides pulled a half-dozen packets of white ropes from their pockets. The head guard removed Poirier's straightjacket. This operation took quite a while because the fasteners were difficult to undo. It was quite unsettling. Those who were holding the lamps couldn't keep their hands from trembling. Finally the straightjacket was removed. Poirier remained as still as before.

Restraints were applied. His feet were loosely tied together in order to allow him to walk. Then his elbows were forcefully drawn back and tied the one to the other. That made him sit upright, jut out his chest, and lift his head up. I was no more than a meter away from him at that moment and in an excellent position to observe the terrible effects his impending death had on his face. After two minutes I could see that he had aged twenty years. When the process began, he was thirty years of age. By the time the executioner took the scissors to cut away his shirt collar, he had turned fifty.

Four snips well placed did the trick, leaving his neck bare and covered with a cold sweat. The executioner then cut a lock of his hair and handed it to the priest. It was for the condemned man's wife. In doing it, he had accidently cut the cord suspending a small medal depicting the Holy Virgin. The priest picked it up and, with the prisoner's consent, placed it alongside the lock of hair.

That part was now finished.

The father confessor kissed Poirier and said, "On your knees, my son. Recite your Pater Noster."

Poirier knelt down with some difficulty and recited the prayer, tearfully, almost inaudibly. At that point the executioner, who had left his hat on, removed it and leaned up against the wall. In an irritated voice he said, "Is the Pater finished now?"

The priest looked down at Poirier. "My son, ask God's forgiveness for what you have done."

The prisoner replied in a low voice, "I ask God for forgiveness for my crimes." Then, of his own volition, he recited an Ave Maria in a voice that, strangely, had become strong again.

Monsieur de Paris showed the priest his watch and tapped his finger on the dial to indicate the advancing hour.

The priest lifted Poirier up and murmured, "Be strong, my son."

We filed out. The prisoner walked with a firm stride to the waiting vehicle: the frightful horse-drawn van that had brought the guillotine from Paris, that would carry the condemned man to his death, and would transport his body to the cemetery.

Poirier followed the aides up the steep steps of the van. The two priests climbed up last. The large prison door screeched open, gendarmes surrounded the vehicle, and the cortege started off at a very slow pace. I followed behind.

Ever so slowly we followed the lovely promenade that is called Tour de Ville (Tour of the City). Daylight revealed a stunning morning, droplets of dew fell gently upon the gendarmes' tricorns, and their horses stretched their necks trying to nibble the leaves on overhanging branches.

From time to time a chorus of chirping of birds was heard. Only a few people lined the route. We continued at the same, slow pace. I tried to listen to what was happening in the van, but without success. The prisoner and the priests must have been talking in near-whispers. Did Poirier even notice through the window the beautiful morning that would have no midday for him?

"Present arms!" I heard the command uttered by a deep voice and saw ahead of us a squadron of dragoons whose golden helmets gleamed in the sunshine. In the center of them was the guillotine. The van pulled to a halt. I stationed myself next to the basket into which the head would fall, a bit to the left to be able to see everything.

The van's door was opening. The crowd shuddered. Some two thousand people had gathered there. The condemned man climbed out. He had aged even more in the interim, but he was still holding strong.

He was being supported on either side by the two priests. He kissed each of them and fell to his knees. All hats in the crowd came off at that point, except those of the executioner and his aides. The executioner stepped away to give him room. Poirier recited a Pater Noster and an Ave Maria, kissed the crucifix, and then groaned, "Forgive me, my God. You are so innocent and I am so guilty."

Monsieur Roch slammed his hand down forcefully, grasping Poirier by the shoulder. The sound of it was heard throughout the crowd. Poirier got up. The aides seized him roughly.

"Pity," Poirier gasped. "Have pity on me!"

There was a snap. The upper portion of the lunette had clamped down. Then there was another, louder sound. It was over. Already the first aide was tossing the hideous grimacing head into the basket. There was almost no blood.

On the square a terrified silence reigned, disturbed only by the tic toc of the mill I had noticed during the night.

That's enough horror for the time being, don't you think? So I'll describe ever so briefly the dead man's burial. His body, without being placed in a coffin, was thrown into a deep ditch and covered with pebbles. The first ones that fell upon the flaccid flesh bounced about like rubber balls.

My goodness, I assure you that on the trip back to Paris my thoughts were far from gleeful. All the way to Versailles, at least, I relived the prisoner's funerary preparation, the sight of the dreadful machine that can cut off a head in an instant, and especially the scene at the cemetery and the tomb that was gorged with flint stone.

Those are memories that come to mind far more often than I should like.

CHAPTER EIGHT
Pierre-Désiré Moreau and Charles Boudas

People have not forgotten the Moreau affair, an affair that was known for a quite a while as the case of the beautiful herbalist of Saint-Denis. Moreau, the owner of an herbalist shop on the Rue de Paris in Saint-Denis, lost his wife to a strange disease. Its symptoms were a low-grade fever accompanied by episodes of spasms and a burning sensation in the throat. A doctor was called in for treatment, after which she seemed to be better. The next day the symptoms returned more severe still. That pattern continued until her death.

Moreau cried incessantly. Then he married Mademoiselle Lagneau, a very pretty young woman who possessed a handsome dowry. After a time the new Madame Moreau fell ill as well, and the symptoms of the malady were exactly the same as those of the first wife.

When the second wife died, rumors surfaced to the effect that Moreau was responsible. The two cadavers were exhumed. The autopsy performed by Doctor Bergeron and the chemical analysis performed by Professor Lhote revealed the presence of an excess of copper in the stomach and intestines of the two women.

A controversy arose, and is still ongoing, concerning copper salts and Moreau's culpability. Some practitioners believe the salts to be harmless, whereas others, Doctor Bergeron first and foremost, assert that they are violently toxic. Doctor Bergeron committed the indiscretion of blurting out in court a damning accusation for which he has been harshly criticized ever since. "I swear," he said, "that man is guilty!"

Despite repeated denials, Moreau was condemned to death. He maintained he was blameless until the end. Before the guillotine, he proclaimed his innocence so persuasively that many people present were moved to believe him. In fact many still believe he was the victim of a judicial error.

Boudas was a carpenter from Batignolles[30] who had murdered a secondhand dealer named Faath in order to steal the man's securities, which he later liquidated in Alsace. He was arrested as soon as he returned to Paris and was executed the same day as Moreau.

---

[30] Batignolles is a neighborhood in the 17th arrondissement of Paris. It is sandwiched between Montmartre and Pigalle.

CHAPTER NINE
The Execution of Pierre-Désiré Moreau and Charles Boudas (13 October 1874)

The day the famous poisoner Couty de la Pommerais was executed, he stepped out of the registry and into the Roquette courtyard. There, he looked up taciturnly at the radiant sky bathed in pale starlight and, in a voice full of melancholy, murmured these words: "Oh, to die on such a beautiful morning."[31]

The morning was more beautiful still on October 13, 1874, the date of the double execution of Moreau and Boudas. Those in the know who waited at the foot of the guillotine recalled vividly the guilty doctor's reflection on that fateful morning. Despite the fine weather, however, relatively few people from the surrounding neighborhoods had gathered in the square, and the police officers were able to maintain control with little difficulty. Actually, there had been much larger crowds the nights leading up to the 13th. But people tired of showing up for an execution that didn't take place as they had heard. In reality, there were no more than three thousand onlookers to bid the two good-bye.

I'll not describe the crowd in detail. It's always the same: workers, carousing night owls, and nauseating, young thugs, several of whom will well end up facing

---

[31] Dr. Edmond-Désiré Couty de la Pommerais was executed June 9, 1864 for having poisoned his mother-in-law (Madame Dubizy) and a former mistress, Madame Pauw.

the guillotine themselves. Additionally, the event usually attracts women and young people who have just enjoyed a late-night supper and who, despite their calm demeanor, feel a tightening of their chests and grow nearly as pale as the paper on which I'm writing.

Between four and five o'clock spirits remained high. There was a constant din of voices, laughter and verbal joisting, sometimes quite ignoble. As five o'clock neared, the voices grew instinctively quiet, as though people had gathered in the room of a dying man.

Some fifty of us were allowed to gather close around the guillotine. Within the circle there were mounted police. Many of us were journalists, of course.

The executioner paced about the machine of death, giving his final instructions in a curt voice tinged with emotion. It was almost time. At five: ten he said, "That's it. It's time."

Monsieur Roch led his five aides into the prison. It was time to wake the prisoner. Here is how it went from there.

When the prison warden, the deputy public prosecutor, and Monsieur Souveras, the head of security, went into Moreau's cell, they found him sleeping soundly on his side. Monsieur Souveras tapped him on the shoulder. Moreau awoke immediately and looked at everyone callously.

"I understand," he said, "and I'd like to get dressed."

He sat up without displaying the slightest bit of emotion and asked for his clothes. After his straightjacket had been removed, he was given the same black trousers he wore to criminal court and his kid leather boots.

"May I please have my stockings?" he asked.

"It's not worth the trouble," came the reply.

"If you don't mind, I'd prefer to have them," the condemned man insisted.

His request being granted, he dressed nonchalantly, taking care to adjust his belt buckle just right. During the entire procedure, he did not show any signs of faltering, nor did he utter a word.

Having donned his trousers, he asked that his frock coat be draped over his shoulders. The rest of us left, leaving him alone with his confessor. Five minutes later he was led out of his cell and headed in the direction of the preparation room.

Those accompanying him took hold of his arms to support him. "There's no use," he protested. "I can walk quite well on my own."

They did not let go, however, and they continued on. He remained silent while his feet and arms were being bound. He looked at the executioners with an expression of indifference on his face, or listened to Father Legros, curate at the Church of Belleville, who was assigned to attend to him in his last moments.

When everything was ready, he stood up and asked to embrace his cell guard. He then said, "Let's get on with it. You'll see that I won't flinch."

"Do you have anything to say?" Monsieur Souveras asked him.

"No, nothing."

While this was happening, Monsieur Claude, head of security, went to the next cell where Boudas was being held. Boudas was awake and was talking loudly and nervously with the guards.

"Ah, ah! It's for today," he said in a sputtering voice. "Well, Justice is going to be guilty of a terrible crime on my account. I'm being led to the slaughterhouse. It doesn't matter, I'm not afraid, but I'm a thief, not a murderer!"

While his straightjacket was being removed and he was fitted with a pair of dark trousers and heavy, iron-clad shoes, he continued to mutter, "I'm innocent, innocent, innocent!"

As he protested his innocence almost without knowing what he was saying, his eyes went glassy and his face contracted rigidly into a fearsome rictus that for all the world looked like a wide grin. Darwin has described scientifically this rictus caused by the involuntary contraction of the platysma muscles of the face, the principal one being the risorius muscle that pulls upward and backward the orbicularis oris muscle surrounding the mouth. That's what gives the agonizing illusion of a terrible grin.

All the while and through the broad grin, Boudas kept repeating, "Innocent! Innocent!"

During the preparation process Boudas made no effort to resist. Although speaking required painful effort, he did manage to tell the executioner several times that he was the victim of a judicial crime.

At six: forty-five the prison gate opened wide. With rapid steps, Moreau strode ahead of the aides who found it difficult to keep up. He did not slow his pace until he was at the foot of the guillotine. He stopped there for a moment, looked up at the blade, and threw his head back haughtily, the muscles in his face placidly relaxed. As he stood there, it occurred to me that he cast a strange resemblance to a well-known engraving of one of the four sergeants of La Rochelle marching to the scaffold.[32]

Having paused briefly, Moreau turned toward those of us standing nearby and said matter-of-factly, in a strong and clear voice without a trace of showmanship, "Messieurs, I am dying innocent."

Then, after having kissed Father Legros rather indifferently, he walked straight to the bascule. The blade fell no more than three seconds later, sending a spray of blood that collected on the paving stones and caused a horrible, collective shudder to run through everyone who had crowded around the death-dealing device.

Several people who had anticipated such a reaction had brought flasks of smelling salts with them. As the flasks were uncorked, a strong odor of ether drifted through the crowd.

Now it was Boudas's turn. He was scheduled to arrive in three minutes. Hearts beat faster in anticipation of his arrival. The executioner's aides quickly sponged off the guillotine and raised the blade once again.

At five: fifty-four, the prison gate opened again. Boudas appeared and walked out at a firm pace, that terrible grin still stretched across his face. He wore a fedora that one of the aides removed as he neared the guillotine.

Father Crozes turned to him and said, "Kiss me, my son."

The condemned man's face contorted completely now, distorting all his features. His eyes began to roll.

---

[32] In 1822 four soldiers were guillotined in Paris for plotting to overthrow the Bourbon monarchy of Louis XVIII. Numerous depictions of them appeared in 1830 as Louis-Philippe was wresting the throne away in the name of the House of Orleans.

He tried to move his lips despite the terrible contraction that immobilized them. He finally managed a kiss that was so loud it could be heard by everyone in the square.

The executioner let Father Crozes know that he was free to go. He then grabbed the prisoner and placed him on the bascule. A horrible scene was about to transpire.

Now in order to prevent the prisoner from moving his head, his neck is enclosed in an apparatus called the lunette. The aides, in placing his head in what is dispassionately known as "the oven," pushed down so hard that his shoulders were partly exposed to the blade.

"Pull him back!" the executioner shouted.

The aides pulled on his legs, but once again they had overdone it. The effect was that the condemned man's chin was now compromised. The executioner himself took over and pushed the man several centimeters forward.

The blade fell. Boudas had not budged during the entire horribly botched affair. What is more, he was able to see Moreau's severed head in the wicker basket below him.

As soon as the execution was over, the two heads were thrown into the large basket where the bodies had been placed. Boudas's head was still grinning, his eyes remained glassy and wide open, his nostrils were pulsating convulsively.

The basket was then placed in the executioner's van. Father Crozes followed in a fiacre, number 148. The gendarmes took the lead and at a quick trot led the cortege toward the cemetery for the executed, the Ivry cemetery.

There then occurred an incident that made a lasting impression on me. The horse of one of the gendarmes was somehow frightened by a bucket and when it shied away it brushed up against the guillotine and in the confusion a gendarme's boots were splashed with blood.

I followed the procession all the way to the cemetery in order not to miss anything. Along the way I observed several women making the sign of the Cross at the sight of the doomful vehicle. One of them was on her knees.

As the procession entered the cemetery, the gates were immediately closed behind it. It had taken only forty-five minutes to travel from the Place de la Roquette. Never have I seen anything so sinister as the corner of the cemetery largely reserved for the cadavers arriving from the Place de la Roquette or Clamart.

Weeds and brush had taken over the rocky area. Long trenches awaited the bleak remains of the decapitated and the dissected. Nary a wreath, nary a flower could be seen, except, at the spot where Troppmann[33] was buried, a small tuft of blue flowers had taken root.

Two of the executioner's aides removed the basket containing the bodies from the back of the van. They checked to see that the heads were with the right bodies. They then dumped the remains into two trenches. The gravediggers aligned the bodies properly. While this was going on, Father Crozes knelt atop a small rise and recited prayers for the dead.

The bodies were claimed by the families the next day and were promptly exhumed.

A final ignoble notation before ending: No sooner had the executions been carried out, than all the newspaper vendors on the Rue de la Roquette began selling a piece titled "Moreau's Lament," a rather stupid thing to

---

[33] See Chapter Two, note 9.

do, if you want my opinion. For those who saw the man die, nothing could have been more sickening.

CHAPTER TEN
Pierre-Louis Bacquet
(31 March 1875)

Pierre-Louis Bacquet's appeal had been rejected and his bid for clemency had been refused. There was no other choice than to get on with the execution. But the Holy Week was coming up, and since Monsieur de Paris never worked during the Holy Week, the execution was delayed. As for Bacquet, the length of the delay convinced him that his request for clemency had been granted. So he began to make plans for the future; he began to dream about the work camp on Devil's Island as you and I would dream of castles in the air.

Now the 30th of March, at four o'clock in the afternoon, the public prosecutor decided that the execution of the murderer of the Rue Hauteville[34] would take place the next day at dawn.

I arrived at the Place de la Roquette at three: thirty that morning. The square was deserted, except for the usual police contingent and the members of the municipal guard who, in their long dark blue coats, ringed the area on horseback.

Since the execution had not been announced in advance, a mere half-dozen curious onlookers watched that morning as the executioner's carpenters went about setting up the guillotine on the legendary stone slabs. Eve-

---

[34] Grison's note: Bacquet had murdered a Rue Hauteville wholesaler, Charles-Édouard Roscher, the 20th of December, 1874.

rything seemed ready at five o'clock, although the device was not quite aplomb and the uprights wobbled a bit when touched. The executioner, who had been watching the workers closely, decided that the problem could be solved by stabilizing it with one's hand while on the scaffold. No further thought was given to the matter.

Daylight had come to the square, revealing a cloudless sky. It was a beautiful day for the "job," as Monsieur Roch called it.

At five: thirty, the executioner was talking with his aides when he pulled out his watch and indicated it was time go into the prison. One of his assistants, to be sure everything was functioning properly, raised the blade and let it fall. It functioned perfectly well, so he hoisted "the sword of justice" again.

The sinister group ambled in by way of the vehicle entrance. As they were going in, I turned and noticed that the bascule that had just been tested was brand new. The bascule is a pine plank whose color stands out from the dark color of the uprights, the black of the basket and the black of the cutting mechanism. Bacquet would be the first to try it out.

Meanwhile, a group of individuals had entered the condemned man's cell: Monsieur Claude, the prison warden, accompanied by the head of security, Monsieur Baron, the local police commissioner, Monsieur Villemez, and a clerk from the prosecutor's office.

Bacquet was sleeping soundly on his back. He merely grunted when the warden touched him on the shoulder. When the warden shook his shoulder, he awoke and yawned.

"Bacquet!" Monsieur Claude said.

The prisoner, seeing through heavy eyes the several people surrounding him, shuddered visibly and sat up.

Fully awake now, he clenched his teeth and looked about somewhat wildly.

The warden spoke again. "Bacquet, it is time to summon your strength."

"Both your appeal and your bid for clemency have been denied," Monsieur Claude added. "Get up. Today is the day."

"All right, I'm getting up," Bacquet said in a weak voice.

And with a composure that none of them expected, he got up and put on his pants and his shoes. He then slipped into a brown, woolen coat, saying that it must be cold outside. From his table he took a pipe already filled with tobacco. He took a piece of paper, twisted it, and lit the end using the flame of an oil lamp.

When the pipe was lighted, he said. "I'm ready."

The others left him alone with Father Crozes. They talked for four or five minutes. It appears that Bacquet repeated the confession that he had made after being transferred to La Roquette.

Bacquet was then led to the registry room where the executioner and his aides were waiting. Upon seeing Monsieur Roch, he stopped and stared at him with a look of desperation, a look that became mournful and then no more than a blank stare.

Inside, he was seated on a stool. The aides cut away several tufts of hair from his neck, those they describe as interfering with the alignment, meaning those that might hinder the blade in its downward trajectory.

When Bacquet saw he was about to be bound, he said, "Oh, don't bother with that. I'll be just as cooperative as I am now."

"It's the rule," the executioner explained gently.

Bacquet allowed his legs to be bound without saying anything further. When his arms were pulled back to be tied, as is the custom, he spoke up. "Don't tie me too tight. I know it's not for long, but there's no use hurting me."

With two snips of the scissors, his shirt collar was cut away, again according to the rule. Bacquet's coat was slipped over his shoulders, and the ensemble was about to set off to the guillotine.

"I'd like to say a few more words to the priest," the prisoner said.

He was shown into a nearby cell with Father Crozes. Nothing out of the ordinary occurred during the conversation, which lasted no more than three minutes. On his way out, however, Bacquet had a few words to say to the warden, words that should not be made public.

In the interim, a number of people, not more than two hundred at the most, had come onto the square where the guillotine was still cordoned off by mounted police.

At five: fifty-three, a noise came from behind the vehicle entrance and the large door opened. One of the aides appeared first, sporting an Alpine hat slightly cocked to the side. Monsieur Roch appeared after him. He was playing with his watch chain as he walked along. Finally, on the arm of Father Crozes who was carrying a breviary, came the condemned man.

Bacquet walked at a hurried pace. I could see his face clearly at that moment. He was a man of thirty-six years of age, light blond hair, a small frame, and highly sculpted facial features that vaguely resembled the face on those famous carved pipe bowls.

He stopped a few feet from the guillotine, looked at the blade for a moment, was kissed by Father Crozes, and then, slowly, without being supported, walked to the bascule. The new piece of equipment was rotated, following its usual semicircular path. The upper portion of the lunette came down to enclose the man's neck. Monsieur de Paris nodded at one of his aides to remind him to steady the apparatus with his hand to prevent the wobbling, as I indicated earlier. He did so and then pulled the lever. The blade fell, producing that awful, heartrending sound.

An enormous stream of blood spurted into the air. As one of the aides shoved the body down the plank and into the large basket, I could hear the head thudding into the wicker basket and bouncing about several times.

It was over.

The body was loaded into the executioner's van. As usual, Father Crozes climbed into the number 148 fiacre that had been reserved for the occasion, and the cortege set out for the Champs-des-Navets cemetery, led away at a fast trot by the mounted gendarmes.

A half hour later, the guillotine was almost completely disassembled and the aides, covered with blood, were removing their attire.

There were a number of journalists present. I can honestly say that all of us were extremely moved by Bacquet's execution, more so than any of the other executions we had witnessed, certainly more so than the double execution of Moreau and Boudas.

His was the execution of a little-known criminal whose case had received relatively little newspaper publicity and which took place in the presence of only a handful of people. And yet without ceremony or fanfare, or even any distinguishing detail, there was something particularly lugubrious about its absolute banality. Without fear of contradiction, I can assure you that all my fellow journalists felt just as I did.

CHAPTER ELEVEN
Toussaint-Léon Gervais, a.k.a. The Bois-Colombes Murderer

There was nothing extraordinary about the crime committed by Toussaint-Léon Gervais. He lived in Moulin-Joli, near Colombes,[35] with a widow, a middle-aged, wicker basket and trinket merchant from Alsace who hawked her wares over the countryside.

Monsieur Gervais had set aside some money with the specific intent of being able to afford to marry a younger woman. Of course, before he could do so, he would have to get rid of the "old" one.

So what did he do? He dug a hole in his cellar. Then, one fine day, he picked a fight with his mistress, strangled her, and threw her body into the grave he had prepared.

To people who missed seeing her the next day he explained that Madame Bonnerue had gone off on a trip that would last several months and that she would return in the spring. The date was November 4th, 1875.

With great gallantry a few days later, Gervais offered to one Mademoiselle Jacquin an engagement gift consisting of, in addition to his future prospects, a watch, a ring, and a dress, all belonging to the dead woman.

---

[35] Colombes is a Paris suburb located six miles to the northwest of the city's center. Grison does not say so, but the public record indicates that Gervais was a *chiffonnier*, that is to say, a rag and bone man.

They married, and the two settled in to their new lives. Now one day when a neighbor inquired about the whereabouts of Madame Bonnerue's parrot, the bride thoughtlessly replied that it had been sold for fifty francs. That, plus the rather exorbitant spending in which Gervais had been engaged of late, caused the neighbors to suspect foul play and to believe he had murdered Madame Bonnerue.

They took their suspicions to Monsieur Monentheuil, the police commissioner of Courbeville. Monsieur Monentheuil called Gervais in for questioning. After a great deal of hemming and hawing, Gervais concocted the explanation that Madame Bonnerue had fallen in the cellar and that for fear of being hassled by authorities, he decided to bury her where she fell. He led the police to the cellar where the body was disinterred.

An initial examination revealed no injuries. However, a strange circumstance led officials astray. A large number of ranunculaceae[36] of the most toxic sort was found at the Gervais residence, along with a toxicology book dog-eared to the page discussing poisonous plants. That, of course, led to the suspicion that Madame Bonnerue had been poisoned. The autopsy and a chemical analysis of the intestines, however, turned up nothing incriminating.

"There, you see, I was right all along," Gervais told police.

The investigating magistrate was about to release him when Monsieur Macé, presently director of security but judicial delegations commissioner at the time, asked for a few more days to follow up. What then occurred

---

[36] Commonly known as buttercups.

will remain as one the most ingenious investigations in judicial history.

Gervais said that, finding Madame Bonnerue dead, he then dug the grave. Monsieur Macé set out to prove that the grave had been dug beforehand and that, consequently, not only was there a criminal act, there was also premeditation.

Here is what his suspicion was based upon. Monsieur Macé noticed that, above the hole in which the victim had been buried, a beam showed traces of being burned. Now on the spots where the beam was singed, there were a number of dead ladybugs that had not died after laying their eggs as they usually do but that were killed by the same source that had burned the beam. The proof was that the ladybugs still carried their eggs. Therefore, the beam had been singed well before the month of November, otherwise the offspring would have already been in the larva stage or perhaps even the nymph stage of development. Hence, the beam had been burned by the candle that Gervais used to light the cellar while he was digging the grave. It was thus evident that the grave had been dug prior to Madame Bonnerue's death, proving premeditation.

When Monsieur Macé was able to determine the approximate date the grave was dug, thanks to his persistence and entomological acumen, Gervais panicked and confessed everything. He was tried for murder in criminal court the 12th of July, 1876. He was condemned to death.

"Thank you so much, gentlemen," he said when his sentence was pronounced.

CHAPTER TWELVE
The Execution of Toussaint-Léon Gervais (12 August 1876)

For journalists who are obliged by their profession to cover absolutely everything, to be able to withstand absolutely anything without flinching, their sensitivities tend to erode after a certain time. With regard to Gervais's execution, one of my friends had asked to accompany me to the Place de la Roquette. He wished to witness for himself, at least once, the lugubrious spectacle about which he had heard so much. Trusting my experience in the matter, he wanted me to serve as his guide.

It is his impressions that I shall now relate, not mine. If I had listened to him, we would have left for La Roquette as early as midnight. Already at that hour groups of curiosity seekers were headed to the execution site. Who told them an execution was going to take place? The President of the Republic had approved the order of execution no earlier than two: thirty that afternoon. At two: thirty-five a telegram informed the chief prosecutor. Only then were official requisitions sent in secret to the following offices or individuals: police headquarters to provide security, the commander of the gendarmerie to dispatch a squadron to serve as escorts, the carpenter assigned the erection of the guillotine, the warden, the court clerk, the priest, and finally the executioner himself. Monsieur Jacob, head of security, received the order at seven o'clock that evening and Monsieur Roch at eight o'clock. Only a handful of journalists were forewarned. Despite all that, the ever-watchful public was on the march to the Place de la Roquette.

I explained to my comrade the uselessness of leaving so early. Indeed, at two: thirty in the morning police had evacuated the square and had herded onlookers onto the Rue Gerbier, the Rue de la Vaquerie, and the Rue de la Roquette, allowing only authorized personnel to remain near the prison. Only then was it propitious to show up.

We arrived at two: fifteen. The crowd, which had been kept in check by the police, formed a thick cordon at the entrance to the square. Women and children pushed their way forward in order to get a good view. People chatted, laughed, and carried on as though characters in a comedy. The only thing we didn't hear was that inevitable cricket sound, *cri-cri*, that was so popular at the time.

We worked our way through the crowd until we came to a policeman to whom we showed our press cards. He accompanied us to the prison door where two vehicles were parked and from which men dressed in work clothes were removing pieces of wood painted brown. It was the guillotine already under construction.

In fact it was the new and better guillotine that Monsieur Roch called "the jewel" because of its simplicity and easiness of construction. All the pieces were numbered and held together with bolts. That avoided the legendary, frenetic hammering which, for so long, had resounded from the construction site and had been so unsettling for condemned prisoners.

We watched being put into place the two crosspanels that serve as supports and upon which would be planted the vertical uprights between which the blade slides. A tall man with graying whiskers supervised the work closely. He himself inserted a small wedge in order to level one of the panels resting on an uneven paving stone.

"Who is that man?" my friend asked.

"Monsieur Roch, the head man."

It was indeed Monsieur Roch who, chewing on a cigar, examined with the greatest of care the uprights as they were installed, the blade that was attached using a ladder, the wicker basket filled with bran that was placed close to the bascule. He was especially attentive that the water buckets used for cleansing after the event were filled.

Finally, everything was in place. Monsieur Roch pulled the cord and hoisted the blade, readying it for its trip down the grooves. After watching it fall, he scowled. Something was wrong. The heat had caused the wood to warp, and the bowing had disrupted the spatial integrity needed for the blade to fall properly. An aide came to the rescue. He brought a length of wood, took measurements, cut it to size, and then placed it between the two uprights just above the lunette. Monsieur Roch hoisted the blade again and let it slide half way down the track. He manipulated the mechanism to see whether was operating freely. Satisfied now, he gave the go ahead signal.

I looked over at my friend. He was quite pale now, but remained resolved. He had followed the entire operation very closely.

"Is it possible to speak to him?" he asked.

"Of course. It's simple enough."

Just then several other journalists came up to where we were standing. One of them left to shake Monsieur Roch's hand and to ask whether he thought Gervais would cause problems. We followed.

"I don't really know," the executioner replied, "but I don't think so. You know, they are already half dead. I've never had any problems with any of them."

"And do you think he'll address the crowd?" my friend asked.

Monsieur Roch shrugged his shoulders and said rather loudly, "Speak to the crowd? They would all speak to the crowd if we gave them time!"

We also wanted to know what Gervais was doing at the time, so we joined a group that had gathered around Monsieur Jacob, the head of security.

Gervais was asleep. He was convinced that a period of forty days following his filing for appeal would have to elapse before the final decision. Since only thirty-two days had elapsed, he was resting comfortably. The evening before he had had a healthy appetite at supper. Before retiring, he played a game with the guard, a game he won, by the way, and he went to sleep after having said, "until tomorrow."

"Poor fellow," more than one in the group said aloud, forgetting the crime and thinking only about the death that awaited the criminal.

Five minutes after four. A commotion arose. It was the municipal guards arriving, both on foot and on horseback. Monsieur Cransac, commander of the 11th arrondissement contingent, placed each man at an assigned position. At the same time the officers of the Paris brigade stationed their men in the same fashion. We watched a vehicle arrive, the number 148 fiacre. Father Crozes got out and walked to a spot next to the prison wall. Monsieur Jacob, police commissioner Baron, and Monsieur Roch followed the clerk of the court of appeals into the inner courtyard.

All their faces were terribly pale. Silence spread throughout the crowd. The most emotional people who tried to speak to those standing next to them in an effort to calm their nerves found that their voices stuck in their throats.

By sad contrast, a spate of laughter was heard coming from the edge of the square. It was two women who, fresh from a late supper, had come to see Gervais executed and had nearly fallen off the vehicle they had mounted in order to see better.

The crowd parted. A peloton of stern yet superb gendarmes on horseback, the funeral escort, came onto the grounds and encircled the scaffold. The municipal guards fell in behind them and dismounted.

At ten minutes after four, Monsieur Jacob, Father Crozes, Monsieur Bauquesne (the warden), Monsieur Baron, and two guards went into the cell. Gervais was sleeping. A guard tapped him on the shoulder. He opened his eyes. Still groggy, he looked up for a moment before appearing to go back to sleep.

"Gervais," Monsieur Jacob said, "your appeal has been denied and so has your bid for clemency. Be strong. Your time has come."

But the poor man seemed not to understand. He remained on his bed, stupefied, deathly pale, his eyes dulled by the shock.

"That's impossible," he stammered. "You're just trying to scare me."

The guards removed his straightjacket forcefully, then helped him stand up and get dressed.

"Oh, this is impossible," he repeated hoarsely. "Society will be committing a crime."

Father Crozes kissed him and comforted him. The clerk read the writ. Upon the priest's suggestion, Gervais drank a glass of brandy. Then he talked a while with the good chaplain and for the first time listened tranquilly to his words of peace.

The usual preparations followed. While he was being bound, the condemned man asked Father Crozes to turn over to his children the watch and five francs fifty that were in his vest pocket. He appeared calm now.

It wasn't until he felt the cold steel of the scissors under his collar and against his neck that he trembled and muttered, "I am innocent! This is murder!"

In the square all eyes were riveted on the prison gate. People counted the minutes, the seconds. Hearts began to beat wildly. They had come to see a man put to death and now they wanted to see him live. Some relived the tales of yore in which at the very last moment a messenger arrives with a letter in hand, a reprieve.

Just then a uniformed officer made his way through the crowd and stopped at the foot of the guillotine. His uniform was covered with dust. He walked quickly. Everyone watched him move along. Unfortunately, he wasn't the messenger of yore. It was Monsieur Brisoux of the 12th arrondissement who had just commanded his brigade at a fire in the Charonne quarter.[37] He simply wished to report the event to Monsieur Ansart, chief of the municipal police, whom he knew to be present.

The gate swung open. People removed their hats. The pallor of their faces turned ghastly. Some of them felt compelled to hold on to the iron tree grills for support. My friend was one of them.

---

[37] Charonne was a village east of Paris until it was annexed by the city in 1860. Today it is a quarter in the southern sector of the twentieth arrondissement, not far from the Rue de la Roquette.

"Take out your watch," I said to him.

It read four: thirty-eight. Just then the prisoner appeared, preceded by Monsieur Roch, supported by two aides, and accompanied by Father Crozes. Gervais walked steadily, his head turned to the left, his eyes franticly seeking the fatal blade and then looking away. Monsieur Roch grasped him by the shoulder with his large hand.

"No, no, not so fast," Gervais gasped.

The bascule swung into position. However, despite the wooden support added to align the mechanism, the lunette didn't restrain his neck as tightly as usual. It took him less than a quarter of a second following the release of the blade to twist his neck convulsively and move his head to the right a fraction. The blade struck him at the base of the skull. At the repulsive sight of it people stepped back aghast. Then, in a useless endeavor to display their composure, they feigned a smile.

A mere fourteen seconds had elapsed from the time the prisoner appeared and a mere six seconds from the time Monsieur Roch grasped him by the shoulder.

The body was thrown into the basket and was soon joined by the head. The funeral van set off at a fast trot toward the cemetery, escorted by the mounted gendarmes and preceded by Father Crozes.

CHAPTER THIRTEEN
Baptiste-Joseph Billoir: The Case of the woman cut into pieces

This was a case that engrossed all France for many months. It merits being reviewed.

On Wednesday, November 8th, 1876, two children were playing on the bank of the Seine between Clichy and Saint-Ouen. At that spot in the river there were floats installed by the Saint-Denis firm La Maison Souffrice and designed to trap waste material and animal carcasses for conversion to industrial grease and fertilizer at the factory. The children were walking on the floats when one of them spied a large bundle that the lower water level had left exposed. He tried to pull it to him, but the bundle was heavy. The youngster summoned some workers that happened by. They pulled the bundle out of the water and found, wrapped in an old, blue petticoat with floral designs, the head and torso of a cadaver.

They immediately reported the finding to the Clichy chief of police, Monsieur Paul Guénin. A further search was conducted and the lower part of the body was recovered.

The body was identified as being the remains of a woman of some thirty years of age. Her head had been shaved and her stomach cavity had been sliced open and emptied.

The entirety was sent to the morgue. The stir that the discovery caused would be difficult to exaggerate.

For an entire week it seemed that all Paris filed by in an attempt to identify the body of the "Clichy woman."

An investigation was begun. Monsieur Jacob, head of security, assigned his entire investigative team to the case. Even that produced no results. It wasn't that the woman hadn't been identified. She had in fact been identified several times, first as an Arab woman belonging to a troop of performers that had set up a tent along the Route de la Révolte, about a kilometer from Saint-Ouen. Investigators followed up, only to discover her alive and well and plying her trade some fifty miles away.

The following day, neighbors on the Rue Rochechouart identified the body as belonging to the wife of a cobbler who had recently walked out after an argument with her husband. Once again, that woman was soon found alive and well and about to give birth to a child.

While the search for the cobbler's wife was being conducted, a man from Tours indicated that a maid, who resembled the description of the Clichy woman, had gone missing recently. Photographs of the body parts were sent to him. The reply came: there was no doubt about it. It was definitely her. But, of course, the maid turned out to be as fit as a fiddle.

The fruitless process went on and on. One day, a cook from Ville-d'Avry claimed that the dead woman might well be one of her friends.[38] Monsieur Jacob himself went to Ville-d'Avry and brought the woman to Paris. It was ten o'clock at night. Nevertheless, the morgue was opened. Once the cook was in a position to see the body clearly, she began to sob.

---

[38] Ville-d'Avry was a village in those days. Today it is a western suburb of Paris.

"Oh! It is her, it's Clémence. I recognize her face and her flowered petticoat. The poor woman, that's what leading a depraved life gets you!"

Having regained her composure, the cook said that the victim was Clémence Barbari, the mistress of a soldier from Camp Villeneuve-l'Étang. She provided his name. Officers rushed to the barracks. The soldier identified the photograph and the petticoat as well. For more information, he suggested that the authorities contact one of his friends who was stationed in Rueil.[39]

There the same scenario played out. In addition to the identification, the soldier provided an address, the Rue Lamartine in Paris. At that address the concierge stated that Clémence had moved to a new location, 35 Boulevard de Strasbourg.

Monsieur Jacob, beside himself, rushed to Boulevard de Strasbourg. Breathless, having quickly climbed the stairs to the fourth floor, he rang the bell. The door opened. There, standing before him, was none other than Clémence Barbari.

That was hardly the end of it. Authorities had to endure eighty-three false leads of the sort.

Finally, the evening of the 14th of December, a man came in to the Café Charles, located on the Boulevard Ornano, to have his usual demitasse. He was quite pleased with himself because of a purchase ha had made in the center of Paris. It was a copy of the police photograph of the woman everyone had been talking about. He showed it around the café.

Suddenly another patron blurted out, "It's the wife of the decorated man."

---

[39] Today Rueil-Malmaison is also a western suburb.

The decorated man was a seemingly fine fellow who came every evening to drink absinth and play cards, either Piquet or Bésigue.[40] He was called the decorated man because he had been decorated with the Military Medal by the Republic.

It was like a bolt of lightning. Everyone in the café recalled that the decorated man had come in several times with a woman, and she was the woman depicted in the photo.

The police were quickly informed, but no one knew the man's real name. After questioning, one of the café regulars remembered that he lived on the Rue Christiani. At number 14 Rue Christiani, the concierge recognized the description of a former tenant named Billoir and said that he was now living at number 51 Rue des Trois-Frères.

A policeman was sent to the address where he claimed to be a relative of a waiter at the Charles Café in order to feel Billoir out. Billoir gave nothing away, but he did admit that the woman in the photo must be his mistress, Marie Le Manach, the widow Bellanger. He maintained that she had left him in early November and that he had no idea where she had gone.

He was arrested, nevertheless. He insisted vehemently that he knew nothing about the matter. He was so convincing that he was about to be released. The newspapers demanded, however, that the waste pit of the house on the Rue des Trois-Frères be examined for proof of the crime. Authorities took their sweet time. Ultimately, the 15th of December, twenty-two days after Billoir's

---

[40] Piquet is an age-old game played with a deck of thirty-two cards, the 7s to the 10s and the aces. Bésigue is played with a deck of eighty cards, four sets of the 10s to the aces.

arrest, action was taken. The woman's hair and intestines were found in the pit.

When Billoir found that out, he made it known to the warden, Monsieur de Mazas, that he was ready to confess. Monsieur Jacob was immediately summoned to take his confession.

Billoir recounted that on the night of the 6th or 7th of November Marie Le Manach had come home drunk and had broken one of his favorite glasses. For her clumsiness he kicked her in the stomach. She fell down dead. Knowing that he would be charged, he cut her body in two and threw the pieces into the Seine.

Authorities pointed out that his explanation was impossible because Doctor Bergeron's report indicated that the body was bloodless and that the woman must have been cut up while she was alive. The reason being that after death the blood coagulates and ceases to flow. Moreover, no evidence of a blow to the stomach was found on the body.

I am of a mind to believe that both the accused and the doctor were right. Marie Le Manach could have been unconscious and Billoir could have believed her dead. She would have died only after he cut open her stomach cavity. That's why all the blood ran out. As for evidence of a blow to the stomach, it is known that bruising normally appears only a few seconds after a blow and is formed by the accumulation of blood. Because the woman's blood was flowing out of the stomach incision, the evidence of bruising did not appear.

Whatever the case may be, the investigating magistrate, Monsieur Bresselles, first had him appear at the court of accusations because he claimed that he was guilty only of blows and injuries leading to the woman's death. Subsequently, he was tried at criminal court and convicted of murder. He was convicted the 15th of December and sentenced to death.

"It's the doctor who is killing me," he shouted on learning of the sentence, referring to Doctor Bergeron's report.

The 25th of April, in the evening, Monsieur Roch received a document containing the following order signed by the Prosecutor General:

"Tomorrow, Thursday, April 26, 1877, the executor of criminal orders of the Court of Appeals of Paris will remove the prisoner named Billoir from his cell in the condemned prisoners' section and take him, at four: thirty in the morning, to the roundabout of the Rue de la Roquette where he will be put to death in accordance with the sentence rendered by the Criminal Court of Paris the 15th of March of this year."

CHAPTER FOURTEEN
The Execution of Baptiste-Joseph Billoir (26 April 1877)[41]

On the 26th of April, 1877, the epilogue of a drama that had captivated all France for months finally played out: the case of the woman cut into pieces.

The circumstances of the crime had been discussed for months on end. Speculation concerning a clemency degree had also been rampant, to such an extent that when word of Billoir's impending execution surfaced, no one could believe it. Even at midnight of the appointed day, the reporters for the various newspapers on their way to La Roquette talked in hushed tones about the sad spectacle they were about to witness.

"It's impossible," they all said.

It was true, nevertheless. Despite the favorable opinion given by the prosecutor general, despite the intervention of the press, the Field General and President of the Republic did not see fit to commute Billoir's sentence. Everyone thought that Mac-Mahon would not allow the decapitation of a decorated soldier who had served France.

To the contrary, precisely because Billoir esteemed the army, his crime was deemed all the more heinous. Moreover, the jury had made no pronouncement about extenuating circumstances and, not having signed a call for an alternative, had therefore made clear its intention

---

[41] Grison has corrected the date from the 25th to the 26th of April. See Chapter Two, number 67.

to see the death penalty carried out. Maréchal Mac-Mahon therefore allowed the sentence to stand.

But the public did not have any of that in mind. The commutation had been announced, so people thought, and they believed Billoir would be spared. For that reason, the roundabout of the Rue de la Roquette, which would normally have been crammed with crazed spectators from eleven o'clock on, remained almost empty. At midnight there weren't twenty people there. At two o'clock in the morning, Monsieur Roch arrived with his vehicles. As the death dealing device was being unloaded and installed, the reporters milled about around him. Oh yes, there were some women there as well, and along with the comings and goings, the swishing sounds of silk dresses could be heard.

But that did not last long. Brigades from the 10th, 12th, and 20th arrondissements arrived and occupied the perimeter. Members of the 11th arrondissement brigade evacuated the square of all those unable to justify being there.

With his accustomed nonchalance and a cigar in his mouth, Monsieur Roch carried out the last steps of readying the guillotine. As was his way, he verified everything himself, placed wedges under the legs and arranged the accessories symmetrically. A shiver ran through the spectators as they watched him test the lunette and the bascule and then raise and release the blade three times, each time the blade thudding to a stop on the coil springs. He nodded his head indicating that he was satisfied. All was well. We would not have to witness another incident such as the warped track that moved us so dolefully when Gervais was executed.

One of the aides, Monsieur Constant, climbed on a step stool and carefully wiped the drops of dew that had pearled on the long crosspieces. That final touch was of an appalling realism.

While that was going on, soldiers from the Republican Guard, both on foot and on horseback, took their positions in the square and along the prison for youthful offenders.[42] A brigade of police from the central department also arrived as reinforcements. It was four o'clock in the morning. The sun was rising. The appointed hour was nearing.

Now the Gendarmes de la Seine arrived at a trot, their hats worn crosswise, and positioned themselves in front of the other troops and facing the scaffold. Everything was ready.

I looked about the square and the surrounding area for a rapid estimate. There were not even four hundred people present.

I watched a group of people enter the prison: Monsieur Horoch, clerk of the court of appeals who was representing the prosecutor's office, Monsieur Baron, the local police commissioner, and Monsieur Jacob, head of security accompanied by his assistant, Monsieur Villa, along with Monsieur Roch, of course. Monsieur Bauquesne, the prison warden, and the most worthy Father Crozes were waiting for them inside. The warden led the entire group to Billoir's cell, cell number one on the right, where the prisoner was sleeping peacefully. The bright lights woke him. He sat up and rubbed his eyes, dumbfounded. Then he seemed to realize what was happening.

"Oh, excuse me," he said upon seeing Monsieur Jacob.

---

[42] Known as La Petite Roquette.

The head of security had played such a large part in the case, and he appeared rather troubled. I noticed something striking about him. His large, blue eyes, which could stare down anyone he interrogated, were now half-hidden behind a pince-nez that changed his appearance significantly.

"Now my poor Billoir," Monsieur Jacob said as he approached the prisoner, "your appeal has been rejected as has your bid for clemency. Have strength."

"Oh!" he blurted uncontrollably. Then getting a hold of himself, he folded his arms across his chest and turned toward Father Crozes. The priest kissed him. Billoir then dressed quickly. He was offered brandy and wine. Choosing a goblet of wine, he took a sip and turned back toward Father Crozes who offered words of peace.

Billoir was escorted to the registry for the traditional formalities, then bound and turned over to the executioner. The prison's large double gate opened wide. The gendarmes drew their sabers.

Monsieur Roch and his aides were the first to appear. Then, supported by the priest, came Billoir. Supported? No, not really. Billoir had maintained his composure. The old soldier in him shone through. He was marching to his death, resigned, without hesitation. At the sight of the guillotine he did not stare at it numbly as most condemned men do. He moved his head around and up and down, as would anyone who wished to understand what was happening.

Father Crozes had him kiss the crucifix and kissed it himself as well. Then the lips of the condemned man touched those of the priest. Billoir bowed his head and said in a gentle voice, "Good-bye, Father."

At that moment Monsieur Roch turned terribly pale, his cheeks began to twitch. After struggling, he regained his composure, took the prisoner by the arm, continued on to the guillotine, and placed him on the bascule.

It was over!

Just as the blade thudded to a stop, the sound of a bell was heard. The prison clock was striking four: thirty. The execution had finished one minute ahead of schedule.

The aides began their usual scramble. Just then we noticed with horror a flood of blood covering the bascule, the lunette, and the uprights and that was streaming across the paving stones toward the storm drain. Then a strange, fantastic thing happened. An aide threw the body into the zinc-lined basket where the head had fallen. No sooner had he closed the cover, when it opened again and out popped one of the legs.

That lasted only a second. The basket was quickly loaded onto the waiting van. Father Crozes climbed into the number 148 fiacre, whose elderly driver and white horse know the doleful route all too well. The cortege, escorted by five gendarmes, then set off for the Ivry cemetery at a fast trot.

At the cemetery, the guard, who had been forewarned the evening before, opened the gate to the designated section. The basket was carried to the edge of the grave that had been dug during the night. Its contents were dumped haphazardly into the pit.

The van and the gendarmes sped away. The gravedigger threw a few shovelfuls of dirt into the grave before leaving himself. Father Crozes stayed behind, alone.

If, an hour later, you had glanced through the disjointed wooden fencing that surrounds the Champs-de-

Navets section of the cemetery, you would have seen an old priest praying at the tomb of a murderer.

CHAPTER FIFTEEN
The Execution of Ange-Valentin Roux (Versailles, 21 June 1877)

If an execution is an exciting event for the people of Paris, it is even more so for those living in the provinces. Therefore, ever since the denial of the appeal of the three killers of Argenteuil,[43] the residents of Versailles had been in a state of constant alert.

A triple execution is such a rare thing, and there was no doubt that all three would fall to the blade. They had all participated equally in the crime. Alexandre Déon, egged on by Georges-Désiré Lamoureux, had inflicted the knife wound. Roux had pressed his knees into the poor widow's chest to suffocate her. Lamoureux had served as lookout and had helped carry the victim to the cellar. What was more, all three then proceeded to drink and play cards next to her quivering body. How could these monsters not be equally responsible? Because of his age (eighteen), Lamoureux alone seemed worthy of mercy at the ministry where policy dictated that cutting off the head of a child should be avoided. But the jurors, finding the "child" precociously corrupt, deemed him as guilty and as dangerous as his accomplices. They therefore rejected a declaration of attenuating circumstances.

---

[43] Grison's note: Roux, in the company of two other, young thieves, murdered an Argenteuil cabaret owner, the Widow Tartarin. (Argenteuil lies some twenty kilometers north of Versailles.)

Having grown quite tired of legislative squabbles, all Versailles was on the lookout for the execution. Every evening, bands of people awaited the arrival of Monsieur Roch at Vieux-Montreuil.[44] Wednesday evening a bizarre-looking vehicle arrived at the Chantiers railway station. Despite the vigilance of the station master, it was soon discovered that the vehicle contained a number of strange items. Finally, four men were seen going into the Hôtel de l'Étoile d'Or, 73 Rue des Chantiers. One of them was quite recognizable, his picture having appeared so frequently in the newspapers. This time the execution was certain, but for only one of the three, the sentences of the other two had been commuted.

I, of course, had been forewarned. I arrived in Versailles just as a squadron of gendarmes was leaving their barracks in route to the execution site.

People in Versailles were certainly accustomed to the sounds of troops on the move, but this time the reverberation of hooves on the uneven paving stones of the Rue des Chantiers caused shutters to open and heads to appear at windows. Doors opened and soon an entire procession of people had formed behind the gendarmes. The number of people had grown quite large by the time the procession reached Pont-Colbert.

Pont-Colbert is a strange place to hold an execution. It's a bridge located on Route 186 between Gonards Woods and the Porchefontaine racetrack. A large pathway that leads into the woods forms a picturesque junction embellished by grass and moss beyond which lies a grove of tall trees. That's where the scaffold was erected.

---

[44] Vieux-Montreuil is presently an affluent quarter in Versailles. It had been an independent village until 1870 when it was deemed a "faubourg" of the city.

It was there that Poncet, a criminal of legendary stature, lost his head, as did Brûlé, the last condemned man executed by Monsieur Heidenreich, who died himself two weeks later.[45]

Opposite this comic opera scene, a squadron of twenty gendarmes on horseback and twenty on foot was led into position by Captain Legay. Up the way, the noise caused the curiosity seekers to peer out from behind trees and above thickets. They had been hiding there since early evening, like so many wild animals.

The gendarmes cleared the road and herded the onlookers to the side. At one o'clock Monsieur Roch's van came into view. I watched as, piece by piece, the deadly device was unloaded and assembled on the uneven ground. While this was happening, a number of officials arrived in succession: the central commissioner, Monsieur Corajod, three other police commissioners with a squad of municipal police to back up the gendarmes, and the court clerks. A few local dignitaries were admitted to the inner circle to which Captain Legay graciously allowed journalists to gather. As journalists we were placed at their beck and call to answer any questions those gentlemen might have concerning the details of the lugubrious act that was about to transpire. By the same

---

[45] Barthélémy Poncet's exploits included escaping from Cayenne and fighting his way through the Guiana jungle to freedom, only to be arrested again. He escaped again, fled to North America and then to England where he continued his wanton ways. He was tried in criminal court, condemned to death, and executed in Versailles the 10th of February, 1866. Gustave Brûlé was executed in March of 1872. Notice that Grison has once again corrected the name from Brunet to its proper form: Brûlé. See Chapter Two, number 10.

token, they were quite informative themselves. They told us, for example, that two thousand people had congregated at the octroi gate, which was closed at the moment.[46]

All the while Monsieur Roch and his aides were going about their business. A roadwork shed situated opposite the junction served as a center of operations. Once the device was erected, the executioner followed his customary routine of examining all the parts. When he tested the blade each of the usual three times, those present cringed at the sound of it thudding to a stop.

It was three o'clock in the morning. Two hundred men from the 76th infantry brigade appeared on the scene, commanded by a mobile gendarmerie captain. Dawn was breaking. The sun on the horizon tinted the clouds purple, an effect we all would have admired on another occasion. But now, given our present state of mind, the light seemed to concentrate around the deadly machine's blade and form a halo the color of blood. In the early light I could see people in the nearby trees. One of them was perched just above the bayonet of a sentinel. Should he have slipped, he would have quite literally been skewered. Monsieur Roch leaned up against an upright and waited. Next to him, Monsieur Corajod took advantage of the lull to ask him yet another question and to swing the bascule around toward the basket himself. Below, an aide was adjusting the sound-cushioning mechanism.

At that point Monsieur Roch took out his watch. It was time to get the prisoner. The blade was hoisted a

---

[46] The octroi wall was designed to prevent merchants from avoiding taxes on goods brought into municipalities.

final time. A small bench was loaded onto the van that had transported the guillotine and that would be used to ferry the prisoner to the site and to remove his body afterward. The horses pulled away quickly.

In Saint-Pierre Prison Valentin Roux had attended mass and had taken communion. Monsieur Roch oversaw the prompt completion of the remaining formalities. The van then headed back to the guillotine, some two kilometers distant. Four mounted gendarmes led the way. Two others flanked the vehicle on each side, and eight gendarmes on foot followed at quickstep.

A large flood of people was already streaming toward the site. They fell in behind the van as it passed through the octroi gate.

It was now four o'clock. The sun had risen above the horizon. Birds were chirping in the trees. This execution that was about to take place out in the beautiful and joyous country put me very much in mind of a moving story written by Étienne Béquet, *Marie, ou le mouchoir bleu* (*Marie, or the Blue Handkerchief*), in which a man is executed in the sunshine and surrounded by flowers and greenery.[47]

The van came to a stop. The folding steps were lowered next to the guillotine and the priest climbed out. He was quite handsome and wore a long, gray beard. Then the condemned man appeared, just a lad, beardless, pale, ashen. He was nude to the waist and had to be supported. The priest, being sure to block his view of the

---

[47] Étienne Bequet (1797-1838) was a popular journalist and critic who wrote a column for the celebrated *Journal des Débats* for some fifteen years. The story in question appeared in the *Revue de Paris* in 1829.

guillotine, kissed him on each cheek. Monsieur Roux kissed him as well. The priest placed his hand on Roux's head, spoke a few words of absolution, and stepped aside. The prisoner was quickly placed onto the bascule and the blade was released. A long stream of blood spurted into the air, splattering onto the face of one of the aides and onto the white trousers of a customs agent who ran off aghast.

The body was loaded onto the van. Police Commissioner Collignon and the priest climbed in. The horses broke into a trot. A coffin furnished by the City of Versailles had been delivered to the cemetery. I overheard one of the gendarmes behind me say, "What a shame. He would have been twenty years old next October."

CHAPTER SIXTEEN
Jean-Pierre Welker: The Murder on the Rue Nationale

At number 17 Rue National in the 13th arrondissement, there is a small hotel run by Monsieur and Madame Hurel. It's a modest establishment within the means of the many working-class residents of the quarter.[48]

On Tuesday, May 20th of 1877, a young man showed up at the hotel and asked to rent a room. He registered under the name of Pierre Welker, a twenty-year-old day laborer from the Haut-Rhin region of Alsace. He had selected the hotel, he said, because he was acquainted with the neighbors who lived at number 15, Monsieur and Madame OEkerlé.[49] Beforehand, he had resided with a relative of the OEkerlés and had visited the family on several occasions. It was Madame OEkerlé who presently did his laundry for him. Welker paid the week in advance and spent the night in a small room at the end of the hallway on the second floor.

The following morning he went out, saying he was looking for work. He didn't return until the following Friday at noon.

---

[48] The Rue Nationale runs parallel to the Seine between the Boulevard Vincent Auriol and the Boulevard Messina of today's Paris.

[49] The public record lists the family name as Eckérlé.

"I've found work at La Villette," he said. "I've been unloading boats for Monsieur Say with a friend of mine who put me up the last couple of nights."[50]

Welker went out again.

He came back at four o'clock. He arrived along with the elder of the two OEkerlé daughters, eight-year-old Marie-Joséphine. Madame Hurel, who knew the girl well, believed she was headed for the courtyard to play with her little friends, as she often did, and didn't give it another thought. She didn't find anything suspicious about Welker's presence since he knew the OEkerlé family.

Welker went out for dinner at six o'clock without speaking to anyone.

All the while, Madame OEkerlé had been looking for her daughter. No one in the family had seen her, nor had any of her playmates.

"But wasn't Titine with you earlier in the courtyard?" Madame Hurel asked.[51]

"No, she never arrived."

Just then a disturbing thought came into Madame Hurel's mind. She recalled that little Joséphine had come in at the same time as Welker. She also recalled the strange, contorted look on his face as he went out to dinner and when he went up to retire.

Doing her best to hide her troubling suspicions, she said to her husband, "Why don't you go look in the room of the new guest?"

---

[50] La Villette is a quarter in the 19th arrondissement. Today it extends just beyond the Boulevard Périphérique.

[51] Titine is the feminine diminutive of names ending in –ine (e.g., Catherine, Justine, Clémentine and, in this case, Joséphine).

Monsieur Hurel knocked on the young man's door.

"Who is there? What do you want?" Welker shouted from inside. "I'm in bed and can't come to the door."

"Have you seen Titine?"

"No, don't bother me!"

Monsieur Hurel went downstairs and came back with Monsieur OEkerlé. After a lengthy back-and-forth, Welker finally stuck his nose out, asked what was going on, and appeared to block the doorway. The two men pushed him aside and began to look around the room. At that time they had no concrete reason to suspect anything. Monsieur OEkerlé who knew the young man well and believed him to be "a good boy," thought that little Titine may have been frightened of being scolded and had hidden in Welker's room.

The room was small. It wouldn't take long to find her if she was there. The two men looked around and moved closer to the bed. As they did, Welker tried to flee. Monsieur Hurel grabbed him and held him fast. At the same time Monsieur OEkerlé's foot brushed up against something under the bed. When he looked under it saw the feet of a child.

"Ah! You're hiding under there," the father said, his voice full of joy. "You can come out now, little darling, we won't scold you."

As he was talking to her, he reached down and gently pulled her out from under the bad. To his utter dismay, he discovered his daughter's dead body.

Little Joséphine had been strangled with her jump rope, the jump rope with the mahogany handles that her mother had bought her the week before.

Unfortunately, the true motive of the murder was even more odious. A quick glance at the body told the men all they needed to know.

It is quite amazing that, given this horrendous revelation, the father had the self-control to keep from strangling or even ripping to shreds the monster who had committed such a revolting crime.

The OEkerlés live on the ground floor, on the left, at the end of the courtyard. The child had been placed on a bed, dressed in the same clothes she was wearing at the time of the attack. At the foot of the bed the parents mourned, the father somber, mute, and grimacing, the mother crying into a handkerchief. When they were told that the authorities had come for the body, Monsieur OEkerlé stood up abruptly and defiantly stationed himself in front of the body. The mother remained on her knees pleading with the men not to take her daughter.

The men had to reason with the parents, had to make them understand that the law required the measure, and had to formally promise that the body would be returned to them. Finally, the father, formerly a soldier in the Crimea and Africa, gave way to legalities, and the body was taken away.

Word of the crime had spread quickly. Such a large crowd had gathered at the OEkerlés' door that it was difficult to remove the body.

When the two employees arrived at the morgue pulling the little trolley that is used for such sad occasions, the people who had gathered there saw them coming in their red-vested uniforms and crowded around the entrance so tightly that the police had difficulty creating a pathway for them.

Joséphine's body was finally checked in to the morgue. The autopsy was eventually performed by Doctor Delens.

I went to view the body a few hours later at the morgue. Little Marie-Joseph was in fact somewhat tall for her age. Her hair was cut short, making her look a bit like a boy. Her face and neck bore the scratches inflicted upon her by her beastly murderer.

I shall refrain from relating the frightful details the autopsy revealed. It would simply be too repulsive. Moreover, if the rumors that were rampant in the 13th arrondissement were true, this was not the first crime of the sort that Welker had committed. Several children in the quarter had been groped or assaulted by an unknown individual, and it was very possible the man in question was Welker.

CHAPTER SEVENTEEN
Marie-Joséphine's Funeral

Little Marie-Joséphine OEkerlé's burial took place three days later.

At nine o'clock in the morning, the morgue delivered the body back to number 15 Rue Nationale. Monsieur OEkerlé had been apprised and was waiting outside. He recognized his daughter immediately. The little casket was closed and carried into the second of the two rooms that constituted the unfortunate family's living area.

Madame OEkerlé came into the room and asked to kiss her daughter good-bye one last time. Her husband had to invent all sorts of nonexistent regulations to prevent her from opening the casket and suffering an emotional shock that might well prove fatal. Monsieur OEkerlé had been sick with fever all winter. Madame OEkerlé had undermined her health by working tirelessly to provide for the family.

As I have mentioned, the OEkerlés' residence was located on the left at the end of a corridor. No sooner had the body arrived than the entire corridor had filled with people. One after the other they walked by the little casket covered with flowers. It was lighted by two simple candles and adorned by a copper crucifix. Those who stopped to pray before the little casket made for a heartrending spectacle; many were poor and in ill health themselves. There was a great diversity among them, too. They came from various walks of life, including the types who are usually found in clubs and those who are the first to show up at an uprising. Yet now they all appeared serious and dignified as they dipped their boxwood boughs into their two-sous glasses of holy water and shook them above the casket before making a large sign of the Cross.

They filed by for two hours, in silence, without the grousing and pushing and shoving that normally accompany a gathering of working class people. Exceptionally, at the casket, the indignant voice of a mother could be heard lamenting the child's fate while clasping a child of her own.

At around eleven o'clock an old rag and bone man kneeled at the doorstep. His beard was bristly, his hair in tangles, his clothes in shreds. He wiped the tears from his face with his calloused hand and murmured, "Poor lil' chick, not to fear, Justice will do you right."

As time went on, the ever-growing crowd spilled out beyond the Rue Nationale. It was a strange crowd of bare-armed women and men in their work aprons. They streamed out of the workshops to pay respect to the modest procession and the little girl for whom so many tears had been shed. It was Monsieur Duplessy, mayor of the 13th arrondissement, who assumed the expense of the burial. He had come the night before to inform the family and to express his condolences. Neighbors also came by to express their sympathies.

As I was waiting for the hearse to arrive, a neighbor related a moving anecdote. "Early on the first of June I also lost my little daughter who had been sick for a while," he began. "OEkerlé, who is my compatriot and close friend, came to shake my hand and to offer to spend the night with me next to my dear child. We aren't rich, but I did decide to write by hand a few announcements myself. It was little Marie-Joséphine I asked to deliver them to the neighbors for me.

"She was so pleased to accept. Each time I would write an address, I would tell her where to take the announcement and off she would go. At about four:thirty in the afternoon, I noticed that she had not returned.

"When I finished my sad task, I went downstairs to see whether Marie-Joséphine would be able to deliver the rest of the announcements and to ask her father to come spend the night as he had suggested. I discovered OEkerlé holding the child's defiled body in his arms. It must have been while she was delivering my sad letters that the monster chanced upon her.

"And when I think," the man went on to say, "that the poor little girl had prepared a wreath of white roses for her friend's funeral . . . I have to tell you that I am as grief-stricken by her death as I am by my own daughter's."

The employees from the funeral parlor arrived at noon. The casket was carried out into the corridor where it was placed on two stools. It remained there for a few minutes, covered with flowers and white wreaths. Then it was placed on the funeral float.

Four little girls dressed in white served as pall-bearers. They were Marie-Joséphine's closest friends in the neighborhood: Augustine Dallot, whose mother was a washerwoman at the same address, Georgette Hurel, daughter of the hotel owners, Louise Mazery , and Victorine Maréchal. Following the float were the children of the quarter's Protestant school. Although Marie-Joséphine was Catholic, as was her mother, her father belonged to the reformed church and therefore sent her to the Protestant school.

Then came Monsieur OEkerlé, the image of an old soldier, dressed in his best frock coat sporting the ribbons he had received in the Crimea and Italy, twisting his hat in his hands, and biting his moustache to keep from crying. His two brothers-in-law, Messieurs Kelch and Keller, helped him see to his four children, who were weeping. The mayor, Monsieur Duplessy, walked a step behind him.

In the roadway behind the procession a considerable crowd had formed. At the intersection of the Place Nationale, the police contingent leading the way had to move people aside in order for the procession to pass. The number of attendees was estimated at five thousand.

The funeral service was held in one of the chapels of Notre-Dame-de-la-Gare, Place Jeanne-d'Arc. The space was far too small for the large crowd. The body was then transported to the Ivry cemetery.

CHAPTER EIGHTEEN
The Execution of Jean-Pierre Welker

Jean-Pierre Welker, guilty of the murder on the Rue Nationale, was executed September 10, 1877.[52]

On several occasions I have had the sad duty of bringing to light the stark details of staging the most terrible of all acts of human justice. I have described the arrival of curiosity seekers, the forces of order cordoning off the venue, the erection of the guillotine itself, and, finally, the entry of the corps of the Gendarmerie of the Seine, so beautiful in its highly-disciplined demeanor, and whose appearance sends a collective chill up people's spines because they know it is time to inform the prisoner that his final hour has come.

I shall not repeat those details here, but there is one thing about that morning that I believe worthy of mentioning. It is well understood that people who attend executions out of morbid curiosity must be kept at a distance. Representatives of the press and certain authorized individuals, along with various civil servants and members of the judicial team, are the only people allowed up front.

That particular morning there were perhaps one hundred fifty people grouped around the scaffold that should not have been there. Some of them were wearing a worker's smock, overalls, and a cap. One of them wore a café waiter's jacket and apron. Most of them had a

---

[52] Both the public record and Grison's initial tabulation list the date as September 11, 1877. See Chapter Two, number 74.

pipe clenched between their teeth. In addition, those people who had managed to gain entry by falsely claiming to be journalists had of course taken up positions in the very first row. That meant that the veritable representatives of the press assigned to cover the event had to depend on the intervention of Monsieur Ansart, chief of the municipal police, and Monsieur Siadoux, an officer of the 13th arrondissement, to clear a small space for us to see.

I should add that the presence of a woman within the inner circle was most disturbing. That said, let us now turn to the execution itself.

One thing that was clearly on the public's mind was the condemned man's attitude. For those who were able to obtain details of the closed-door trial, there was little doubt. Following his odious crime, Welker had gone peacefully to sleep on the bed above his victim's body. He related this and other details of the crime quite willingly to the commissioner of police without shedding so much as a tear or showing so much as a feigned sign of repentance. Likewise, he had nonchalantly repeated all the horrible details at criminal court. Welker proved to be vulnerable in only one respect: the fear of death. He burst into tears when he heard the jury's verdict; he burst into tears when he was placed in a cell in the condemned prisoners' section of the prison. But he had shed tears only for his own regard, for his own pain; he never gave a thought, not even for a moment, to poor, little Marie-Joséphine, to the horrible suffering and pain she had to endure because of his odious embrace. Then, as days went by, the thought of death subsided and material existence took over. Welker regained his equilibrium and a certain tranquility. He ate and drank and smoked his pipe and slept without an iota of regret or remorse.

To such a man the announcement that his final hour had come would surely be a terrible shock. And a shock it was.

It was four: forty-eight when Monsieur Roch, having run the final test of the blade, approached police commissioner Baron to say that everything was ready.

It was almost daylight. The stars in the sky grew pale one by one and then disappeared altogether. The decree of execution scheduled the execution for "approximately five: thirty." It was time to wake the prisoner.

Monsieur Jacob, head of security, Monsieur Baron, Monsieur Roch and his aides all went into the prison. After having gone to see that the ubiquitous number 148 fiacre had arrived, Father Crozes went in as well. The warden of La Roquette, Monsieur Bauquesne, and the clerk of records, Monsieur Auroch, waited under the archway.

In cell number 3 the condemned man was fast asleep. Welker thought that the sentence would not be carried out for some time. The decree was dated August 13. He believed like so many others that forty days had to elapse between the issue date of the condemnation and the end of the appeal period. He had no reason to be concerned that day, or so he thought.

Neither the noise of the key in the lock nor the bright light sufficed to wake him. He was lying on his left side facing the wall.

Monsieur Jacob tapped him on the shoulder. Monsieur Bauquesne spoke: "Welker, your appeal has been denied and your request for clemency has failed. You must prepare to die."

From deep in Welker's throat came the cry of a wild beast, both a roar and a groan at the same time. He fell back onto his bed, beset with spasms and clamped his teeth onto the heavy cotton sheet.

Monsieur Jacob was visibly moved by his reaction and grew almost as pale as the prisoner. Nevertheless, he asked, "Do you have anything to say? Do you want something to drink?"

Welker did not reply. He was still shaking. He was lifted from the bed and given his tawny-colored trousers. He tried to balance himself to put them on. Unable to do it, he fell back face down on the bed, crying out all the louder.

The venerable Father Crozes then did his best to console him. To no avail. Welker was not listening. His face turned a deep red, the veins in his forehead and temples bulged. He looked as though he would die before the execution.

He did not die, not yet. But he was only alive physically. His heart continued to beat but his mind was gone. Being in the complete clutches of fear had paralyzed him. When Monsieur Roch applied the restraints to his arms and legs, he did not appear to be aware of it.

"Am I hurting you, my boy?" the executioner asked as he bound the prisoner's wrists. But Welker didn't answer him any more than he had answered Monsieur Jacob or Father Crozes. He was lifeless, mute. The man who was about to be taken to the scaffold was in a cataleptic state.

The business at the registry complete, the guards opened the locks of the large prison gate. The gendarmes already had their sabers in hand. People outside craned their necks to see. Two policemen, Monsieur Dufour and Monsieur Brisou, were the first to get a glimpse of him. They shouted in unison, "He's being carried."

He was indeed being carried. An aide on each side of him had lifted him by the arms and shoulders. His head, which rested on his right shoulder, bobbed up and down, his lifeless legs dragged on the ground.

Father Crozes walked just ahead of him, a crucifix in his hand, and blocked his view of the scaffold. Two loud kisses were heard. The two aides had to exert themselves in order to lift the prisoner, turn him, and drop him onto the bascule with a flaccid thud that sent chills up our spines.

The blade fell. A stream of blood burst forth.

The body was thrown into the basket. The aides started to throw the head in with it. But the angle at which they had to place Welker on the bascule prevented it. The blade had made contact somewhat diagonally, slicing through the chin on one side and part of the shoulder on the other side. Moreover, Welker had an enormous head.

So the head remained for the time being in the basket into which it had fallen. Ultimately, the aides would have to hit the sides of the basket in order to dislodge it.

All that seemed to take a very long time. But it really hadn't. Between the waking of the prisoner and the release of the blade only eighteen minutes had transpired. That is to say, three minutes less than for Billoir.

Escorted by six gendarmes, the body was taken to Ivry for burial. The head, I am told, was claimed by Professor Robin for study at the Paris Medical School.

CHAPTER NINETEEN
Antoine-Joseph Albert: The Malakoff Murder

When Monsieur Pelletier returned home from his job as caretaker of the buildings that formerly housed the café and concert hall called the Tour Malakoff, his wife was not at home. He was seventy years old and his wife was sixty-four. Because during their forty years of marriage the couple had often been separated for various reasons, he assumed that his wife had gone off to spend a few days in Belleville at the residence of a wealthy family that hired her to do chores from time to time. So he wasn't worried and didn't give the matter another thought.

The following Sunday, he traveled to Belleville to see his wife, only to learn to his disbelief that no one there had seen her for six weeks.

Extremely concerned, he went back to Malakoff and expressed his misgivings to neighbors who had no idea where his wife might have gone.[53]

Tuesday the 29th of August, Monsieur Durand, a next door neighbor, noticed that there was a body floating in his well. Assisted by other neighbors, he pulled the body from the well. It was Madame Pelletier.

---

[53] Malakoff, formerly a village southwest of Paris, is today a suburban city. It derives its name from the capture of the "Tour Malakoff" during the Crimean war. Belleville, also formerly a village, is today an area within Paris whose main street is the Rue de Belleville, an artery straddling the 19th and 20th arrondissements.

The body was taken to the morgue where an autopsy was performed by Doctor Bergeron. He determined that the deceased woman had been strangled before being thrown into the well.

Suspicion fell on a twenty-four-year-old, Belgian brick-maker named Albert who lived with the Pelletiers and who had seemed rather despondent recently. The young man had in fact disappeared and along with him diverse objects of value: jewels and a nickel-silver teapot, among other items. Witnesses remembered seeing him on the Auteuil viaduct, a revolver in his hand and quoted him as saying, "There are days when a person could kill someone for no more than a sou."

It was also learned in Valenciennes, where he had lived for a while, that Albert had been overheard saying, "I've got to get away. Something terrible has happened. I got drunk with a cavalryman who has since been found dead from drowning. I'm afraid I'll be accused of killing him."

Authorities searched for him in vain. He never turned up again. The investigation ground to a halt.

It wasn't until a year later that a Belgian named Albert Dessy, who worked on the docks at La Villette and lived at 21 Rue Argonne, went to the police headquarters in his area and said the following to Commissioner Aussilloux, "Arrest my mistress, Philomène Lavoitte. She's the one who killed Madame Pelletier in Malakoff."

Monsieur Aussilloux undertook an investigation. Dessy told him that he had met Philomène Lavoitte in 1876 when she was working for Madame Pelletier as a steel polisher. He said that she had killed her employer, and both of them had run off together. "I couldn't denounce her," he went on, "because I loved her. And, I must confess, I profited from the theft. Sometime later she was unfaithful to me and left me for another man. Now I'm getting even."

The commissioner placed them both under temporary arrest. Information gathered about the two fully justified the measure. They lived quite well but worked very little. Having moved into the Rue de l'Argonne address, Philomène went to work for her landlady as a maid. She tired of it and turned to debauchery. Soon she was seen wearing fine clothing, expensive jewels, and lace, claiming to have benefitted from an inheritance.

The search of the room she rented turned up a large number of pawn tickets, rags cut from magnificent tablecloths, liqueur cabinets, etc., etc.

Because the Tour Malakoff case had been investigated initially by Messieurs Guillot and Macé, Monsieur Ausilloux turned the two detainees over to them. Upon learning of the transfer, Monsieur Macé exclaimed, "Albert, he's the man we have been looking for so long. How old is he? Twenty-six? Of course. Belgian? He's the one."

He was, indeed. It was Albert Dessy who had been a lodger at the Pelletier residence, who had disappeared the 24th of August, 1876, and who later moved in with his mistress at the Rue de L'Argonne address.

But he denied vehemently having anything to do with Madame Pelletier's death, as did Philomène.

"Sure," Philomène said, "I took those items. All maids borrow things from time to time from their employers."

The denials went on for three days. The fourth day, Dessy asked to speak with Monsieur Jacob, to whom he admitted quite frankly that the two of them had killed the "old woman."

As a consequence, Messieurs Guillot, Macé, and Jacob accompanied the two to the Pelletier residence for verification purposes.

At twenty-six years of age and five feet ten inches tall, Dessy was thickset with broad shoulders and a malevolent look in his eyes. He was wearing a long, blue smock, like the one butchers wear, and a small, straw hat.

The woman was of the same age. She was thought to be quite pretty when she worked for Madame Pelletier. She was wearing a flower-print dress with a violet raincoat thrown over her shoulders. Those who knew her from before found that she had changed considerably, having lost so much weight that they had trouble recognizing her.

The investigators gathered everyone into a room at the Pelletier residence. They sat down at a green-painted table that, formerly, must have been placed beneath an arbor and on which many joyous meals must have been served. Monsieur Guillot sat at the head of the table with Messieurs Macé and Jacob on his right and the secretaries on his left. The suspects sat facing him.

Dessy was frightfully forthcoming. He talked to the investigators about the crime as though it were a social occasion. It wasn't the investigators who were controlling the proceedings. He was doing the honors himself.

Here is, according to him, how the crime was committed.

The 24th of August, at about four o'clock in the afternoon, Dessy called out to Madame Pelletier. "A rabbit has escaped," he said.

"Where?"

"Here, in the cellar."

Madame Pelletier came as quickly as her advanced age and infirmities allowed. No sooner had she arrived in the cellar than Philomène grabbed her by the hair and threw her down on a pile of kelp next to a wall. Dessy leaped into action. He wrapped a rope around the poor woman's neck and strangled her.

Having done that, he left for a moment to get some air. During his absence Philomène dragged Madame Pelletier's body behind a pile of wood, and, to be sure she was quite dead, struck her in the temple with all her might.

Dessy returned, and the couple went about carrying the body away. Albert held the upper part and Philomène the legs. They stopped first outside the external entrance to the cellar and then a second time along the pathway that runs around the buildings. At that point Philomène announced that she had given out and was unable to go any farther.

Dessy egged her on. "Keep going, you lazy wretch, when you commit a crime you have to have the gumption to try to hide it!"

They finally came upon an open exterior window of a room where flat cakes used to be sold to walk-ins. Inside, opposite the window, there was a well. Dessy pushed the body through the open window and, having wrapped the rope under the dead woman's shoulders, lowered it onto the floor. Philomène walked around the building and went inside.

Dessy entered by climbing through the window. Philomène took the body by the feet and positioned it so that the legs were on the edge of the well.

Let's listen to the way Dessy himself described what happened then.

"I had tied the rope solidly below the shoulders so that I could lower Madame Pelletier as gently as possible. Because I am in the habit of respecting the dead, I lowered her carefully."

Philomène interrupted him at that point. "That's not true, messieurs. The no-good scum is lying. Madame Pelletier's skirts got caught half way down. The pig had the barbarity to hit her on the head with a stone in order to speed up the process."

"You dirty b . . . ., you filthy liar! She was the one who kept saying, 'Hurry up, drop the f . . . . . . carcass in the water!'"

During the entire interrogation the two continued to dispute each other's versions in the same vulgar vein. Philomène displayed the greatest cynicism imaginable.

With his story finished, Albert offered to show the investigators where everything happened and to repeat the sequence of events exactly as before, from the beginning to the end.

A considerable crowd had gathered outside. When Philomène saw that, she said boastfully, "Look at all the people watching me. It's a rare thing to see an accused woman." Then, with a smirk, as though a great idea had just occurred to her, she went on to say, "When they get ready to cut me down to size, I'll have such a nasty grimace on my face they won't forget me for years to come."

When they were taken away, the two accused were separated. Dessy was taken back by way of Petit-Montrouge and Philomène Lavoitte by way of the village of Malakoff.

Far from cowering from the crowd that watched her leave, Philomène found it quite amusing to make awful faces at people.

Before leaving, the investigators made drawings and took pictures of the crime scene.

CHAPTER TWENTY
The Expiation

After having been announced several times, only to be postponed, the execution of Albert Dessy finally took place October 25, 1877.

The cold and threatening rain failed to discourage the large crowd that surrounded the Place de la Roquette. In spite of the terrible crime Albert had committed, he had aroused a good bit of public sympathy. People had not forgotten that he had turned himself in, and they hoped that his confession would be taken into account. They also recalled the dignified attitude–appropriate though somewhat pretentious–he displayed at criminal court, an attitude that contrasted singularly with the deplorable comportment and vulgar language of his accomplice. What was more, the extracts of his memoirs that were published by *Le Figaro* had drawn the interest of readers, and, especially given the delays of his execution, many were hopeful that his sentence would be commuted.

Therefore, when the execution was announced in the evening, a large number of people turned up at the appointed site. Within the reserved, inner circle there were a good many more onlookers than usual. It appears that certain newspapers had distributed an exaggerated number of press cards and letters of authorization. That was the only explanation I could find for the extraordinary size of the group next to the scaffold.

Although the execution wasn't scheduled to take place until dawn, that is to say, around six: thirty, it was just after four o'clock when the van carrying Monsieur Roch's instrument of death arrived. Its erection, which I have described several times, took little time and posed no difficulties. By four: thirty it was fully functioning.

For the aides and for reporters, that meant two long hours of waiting, two long hours in the cold morning with emotions rising all the while, as much as we tried to overcome them. In the meantime we talked about the crime and its perpetrator. We wondered whether his attitude would hold, whether he would remain calm and resolved until the end, or whether all that had been so much bravado and would melt away at the sight of the guillotine. We also recalled that he had continued to love the wretched woman who had led him to commit the crime. He had asked to see her before dying. The warden had told him it was impossible.

"Impossible?" replied Albert. "Since when can the dying wish of a condemned man not be granted?"

"I'm sorry. Philomène Lavoitte has already been incarcerated in Clermont."

"Oh, I see," Albert said, and his head drooped in discouragement.

Only two incidents occurred to break the monotony: the arrival of the municipal police and the contingent of gendarmes. One other incident is worthy of mentioning. The legendary fiacre number 148 failed to show up. It was replaced by a luxurious carriage.

A bit later a gentleman in military attire with a gray mustache appeared on the scene. On the order of Monsieur Ansart, he was escorted by police to the center of the inner circle where he would not miss a single detail of the event that was about to transpire. Subsequently, I was informed that it was Lieutenant Colonel Vincent of the London Metropolitan Police.

At long last six o'clock had come. Monsieur Roch paced back and forth and looked at his watch. He nodded his head in relief. The long wait had weighed on him as well. Someone nearby said in a voice loud enough for Monsieur Roch to hear, "It appears that Albert is going to make a speech."

"Once he's in my hands, I'll see that he does no such thing," Monsieur Roch replied in his distinctly southern accent. He then followed Monsieur Baron and Monsieur Jacob into the prison. The warden, Monsieur Bauquesne and Monsieur Auroch, the clerk of records, were waiting in the courtyard.

They found Albert in his cell sound asleep. The warden tried to wake him. The prisoner half-opened his eyes and looked around for a moment. But sleep overtook him again and his head fell back onto the pillow.

The warden shook him gently. "Look, Albert, you must wake up."

This time he woke up fully, sat up, and awaited the fatal message he was about to receive.

"Your appeal has been denied, as has your plea for clemency. You need to prepare to die. Have strength."

The prisoner's eyes dilated somewhat. Then in a calm voice, he said, "Yes, yes, let's get on with it. Courage, yes, of course. But I was really hoping to sleep longer my last night, you know."

Getting out of bed, he began dressing. As he was putting on his trousers, he spotted the deputy brigadier of surveillance standing behind the police commissioner. "Well then," he said, looking directly at the man, "has the color gone from my face?"

Although the prisoner's face was in fact pale, the man shook his head no.

"That's because going to meet my maker, I have a clear conscience," Albert declared with his usual touch of bravado. "I was forthright in turning myself in, and I shall be just as forthright in facing death. I don't ask for any pity in this world, only in the next world. Perhaps this last request will be granted."

Albert was asked whether he wished to eat or drink. He declined but asked for permission to smoke a cigarette. Permission was granted, but he didn't take advantage of it until he had taken ten minutes to speak with Father Crozes. That finished, he rolled the tobacco in the paper and lit the cigarette.

When he was again urged to be strong, he shouted, "I won't be lacking in courage! A while ago I was sleeping innocently. And now I am going to sleep for eternity."

It was time to go to the registry to deal with formalities. Before leaving, Albert asked permission to embrace the deputy brigadier and the man who had been his personal guard during his stay at La Roquette.

"You both have been the best of citizens," he told them as he embraced them. "Please give me the kiss of peace and farewell."

He then turned to Monsieur Jacob. "And you, Monsieur, will you allow me to shake your hand?"

"Of course, my friend," Monsieur Jacob said, visibly moved. "And I hope the courage you are displaying now will not abandon you."

The formalities at the registry having been completed, Monsieur Roch took charge of the prisoner. Albert shuddered as he felt the rope that would bind him touch his skin.

"Am I hurting you?" Monsieur Roch asked.

"No," Albert blurted, trying to maintain his self-control. "Besides, I deserve to suffer a great deal in order to pay for the evil things I've done to others."

While the prisoner was being prepared, Father Crozes read a long statement that Albert had prepared the day before and titled "My Repentance." It was a sort of epilogue to the memoirs that had been previously published. The style was rather uncertain. The text itself constituted a view from above, the struggle between good and evil, etc. Albert listened with a degree of satisfaction. Then he got up from the stool on which he had been sitting and, looking quite solemn, lifted his eyes to the heavens and said the following words:

"I ask for your forgiveness, messieurs. I ask forgiveness for all those who have done me wrong and for the wrong I have done to others. Let's get on with it!"

It was daylight now. The gendarmes stood with saber in hand. At six: twenty-three the prison gate opened. Father Crozes walked backwards in front of Albert, blocking his view of the guillotine. The prisoner's eyes searched upward, over the priest's head, seeking the blade.

"Don't look," Monsieur Roch said.

But the prisoner had seen it. His face turned quite pale and an expression of fear crossed it. Nevertheless, he maintained his pace. Near the scaffold he stopped to give the priest a long kiss.

"Come now, come now," Monsieur Roch insisted, as he pushed Albert forward.

Albert arched his back as though to resist. Perhaps he was being true to his theatrical nature and wished to make the speech people were talking about. But he didn't have the time. The aides seized him and forced him onto the bascule.

Then we heard Albert's impassioned voice cry out, "Lord, my God, forgive me!"

The bascule swung into place. Though the prisoner was tightly secured, his muscles revolted instinctively and jerked about. The lunette finally in place, the blade was released.

At that precise moment, all of us there witnessed a strange coincidence. As though a coup de théâtre, the rain began to fall. Only minutes later, the van carrying the cadaver was on its way to Ivry.

People were surprised at the little blood that issued from the beheading. The uprights were hardly touched at all.

As it turns out the phenomenon is easily explained. The prisoner was not high in color to begin with. Being of an excessively nervous nature, and given his extreme pallor, it is evident that on the scaffold his blood drained away from his head and was drawn to his innards.

The Paris School of Medicine had requested the body in a memo to officials, who were pleased to oblige. Professors at the school were anxious to receive the cadaver. They had gathered together at six o'clock that morning to decide which experiments would be conducted when it arrived at about seven o'clock.

Unfortunately, the police commissioner had not been informed of the arrangement. So, as usual, the body was buried at the Ivry cemetery.

Let me quickly add that for Albert a new procedure was inaugurated. Heretofore, the bodies of condemned prisoners had simply been thrown into an open pit. After five or six years, when virtually no trace of the cadaver remained, the site was spaded up and turned over for future use. Henceforth, police authorities had decided, a pine coffin would be provided.

CHAPTER TWENTY-ONE
Luigi Teofilo Corsinesco
(An Execution at a provincial facility, January 4, 1878)[54]

Attending an execution in Melun in mid-January when the temperature is a mere ten degrees Celsius is hardly a plum assignment.[55] The last train from Paris leaves at eleven: ten at night and arrives at the administrative seat of the Seine-et-Marne at twelve: thirty in the morning. Because the sun does not rise until seven: thirty at that time of year, that meant I had seven brutal hours to wait before daylight.

The facts in the Corsinesco case are well known. Originally from the Piedmont region of Italy, he came to Paris to look for work, became involved in an altercation at a sleazy dance hall, knives were drawn, and in the melee he wounded a policeman. For his actions he was sentenced to five years in prison in Melun. In jail his unruly character made adjustment to the discipline of prison life impossible. He was punished for his conduct on several occasions. Now one individual did have an ever-increasing influence on his behavior: another inmate of a decidedly feminine allure, one of those hybrid creatures

---

[54] The public record lists January 5th as the execution date. Grison had Gallicized the condemned man's name. The original Italian form has been reconstituted. See Chapter two, number 77.

[55] Melun lies some forty kilometers southeast of the center of Paris.

that are responsible for rampant perversions in our large cities and who, unfortunately, are well represented in our penal colonies and prisons. The person in question was named Le Bigot but known by the strange nickname of Queen of the Brushes, which stemmed from his assignment to the prison brush-making shop.

Very soon, friendship turned to passion–fierce, uncontrollable, obsessive–in a word, "Italian" passion. One day Corsinesco came to believe that another prisoner by the name of Robin had caught the eye of his "beloved." From that day on it would only be a matter of time before Robin would pay with his life. The night of the twelfth and thirteenth of July, Corsinesco stabbed his rival three times.

When the revolting details of the crime were learned at court, Corsinesco's fate was sealed. The jury took no pity. He was condemned to death. He harbored no illusions about what would happen to him, nor did any of the other inmates. One day, as a work crew was busy digging a trench in the middle of the prison courtyard, an enthralled inmate broke the rule of silence and shouted, "Look! That's where the guillotine will be. We'll get to see the whole thing tomorrow. What good luck!"

As it turned out, it was simply a gaslight that was being repaired. But for two days the entire prison population was on pins and needles in anticipation of the wonderfully horrible event prisoners thought would take place under their very eyes.

The third of January I received my orders. By one o'clock in the morning I was standing on the Quai de Courtille, an area thirty meters in width sandwiched between the Seine and the prison gate.

That's where the execution was to take place. Ordinarily, the prisoner would be taken to the city jail and executed in the designated area there, the site of the June 1873 execution of Servain, the twenty-year-old convicted of patricide.[56] But because Corsinesco had murdered a fellow prisoner, it was decided that he would be guillotined next to the prison as an example to the others and that a certain number of inmates would be allowed to witness the execution, under close guard, of course.

The area outside the prison was empty, with the exception of two women (women can be so audacious!) who kept peering through the iron bars in the prison gate to no avail. All was quiet inside.

Little by little, groups of curiosity seekers strolled in. By three o'clock when the first detachment of troops arrived, there were so many onlookers that it took some time to clear the area. It was common knowledge that Monsieur Roch had arrived at noon the day before and had lodged at the nearby Hôtel de la Ville de Meaux. It was also known that he would have to go to the railway station in the middle of the night to fetch his van and transport the guillotine to the execution site. People wanted to watch the instrument of death being assembled. But the orders were clear. Spectators were forced to cross the Seine and watch the death dealing from the quay on the opposite bank.

While that was going on, two urchins were spotted perched high in a poplar tree and were defying orders to come down. Neither cajoling nor threats had any effect.

---

[56] Once again Grison is at odds with the public record which lists the execution date of Jean-Napoléon Sévin (not Servain) as the 9th of April, 1873.

The more authorities insisted they acquiesce, the higher they climbed. After a while, those in charge simply gave up and allowed the two to retain their ringside seats. The boys were not about to relent after the effort they had expended. They had been in that tree since ten o'clock the night before and would have to remain there in the cold and the numbing mist rising from the river until eight o'clock that morning.

Clocks struck five: thirty. Monsieur Roch arrived with his famous van which, in contrast to its function, was covered with beautiful pearl-like droplets that sparkled in the glow of the lanterns. The installation process got underway. The aides placed the four crosspieces on the uneven ground and took great pains to wedge them into level position. They were about to install the uprights when they noticed that the scaffold would be much too close to the main gate opening onto the walkway where the inmates were to be placed. They would have to move it back. With a sigh, Monsieur Roch agreed and oversaw its repositioning ten meters farther back. It was another glitch that delayed the process a good twenty minutes. There was plenty of time, however. There remained two and a half hours before the fatal hour.

At seven o'clock reveille was sounded. It was the usual time for inmates to head to the workshops. They came streaming out one by one and lined up in the main courtyard. Dressed in their brown jersey coats, they formed vague and shadowy figures in the half-light. They looked like so many giant worker ants teeming out of their nest ready for the day's labor.

But their destination was not the workshops. The courtyard was traversed by two rows of guards, their sabers at their sides and their guns on their shoulders.

Their guns were loaded and their bayonets fixed. The inmates formed four rows, one-hundred men deep, between the two rows of guards who kept close watch.

In the adjacent courtyard, just below the main courtyard, a similar maneuver took place, the sole difference being that the guards assigned there were members of the First Hussars' Regiment. It would have been foolhardy indeed to stage a revolt with such a show of force in place.

In front of the prison gate, fifty inmates, twenty-five on each side, were placed facing the guillotine. Six armed guards were assigned to them. The troops–infantry, cavalry, and gendarmerie ringed–the execution area.

Inside the prison, officials were on their way to wake the prisoner. Monsieur Saillard, warden of the facility, and prison inspectors, Messieurs Laguesse and Bailleul, led the way. Behind them followed the investigating magistrate, the clerk, the deputy prosecutor, a colonel in the gendarmerie, the police commissioner, and the most worthy chaplain, Father Boutroy. Having traversed the adjacent courtyard, the group turned left and, like so many guards making rounds, headed for the cells. Corsinesco's cell was at the top of a stairway.

The prisoner was already up. He had been sleeping no more than six or seven hours a night for the last month. He was seated on a stool at the rear of the cell. At his side were two inmates assigned to keep watch on him. One of them was a one-eyed man of herculean proportions dressed in a white frock-like garment that made him look like an apparition. He was evidently a man whose exemplary conduct had earned him many privileges and was completely trustworthy.

The warden was the first to enter the cell. His voice was filled with emotion. "Well, poor fellow, the clerk has come to tell you that your request for clemency has been denied. The time has come. You will need courage."

"Courage? I have plenty of it."

The clerk began to read. "By decree of the Seine et Marne criminal court . . . ."

The prisoner listened calmly. When the reading was finished, he said, "I understand that I deserve my fate. However, of course, there was no premeditation!"

He got up. The two inmates came forward to accompany him, but two guards intervened. The guards took him by the arms and escorted him down the stairs to the guard post.

He was left alone there with Father Boutroy. The room had two beds and a stove that had been stoked. The prisoner seemed to appreciate the warmth. The priest offered the crucifix. Corsinesco kissed it. In so doing, his beret fell to the floor. He bent over nonchalantly, picked it up, and placed it on one of the beds.

He then turned toward Father Boutroy who was reciting prayers for the dying. With the prayers finished, the warden came in. "Is there anything we can get you, my friend? Is there anything we can do to help you?"

"Me? I don't need anything. I'll be strong. But, you see, what bothers me is to be condemned to death based on the testimony of people who are no better than I am. If it had been honest people, I'd feel better about it."

"What do you expect? You had to be judged by those who were living with you."

"I suppose so. It's all the same in the end. So I'll just have to go along with it."

Time passed. People began to wonder why Monsieur Roch had not arrived. As it turned out, he had been detained by the most trivial of incidents. The pen he was given to sign the receipt of prisoner form did not function. He tried wiping it on his shirt sleeve, but that did not work either. Ultimately he had to ask for another pen. The delay was not long, but for those waiting it seemed an eternity.

Monsieur Roch came in. "Take off your coat," he said good-naturedly to the convict. You'll be able to put it back on later."

Corsinesco knew exactly what was happening. He had witnessed several executions. He knew what to expect. "Good God," he said, "at this point you can do what you like with me."

The coat was removed. It bore the number 21,621. The prisoner was not asked to remove his vest or the brown-woolen, knit shirt he wore beneath it. Everything else went quite quickly.

It was time for the final stage. As the group set off, the warden gave an order, "Berets off!" All the inmates obeyed immediately. At the gate the same order was given to the inmates selected to watch the execution, with the same immediate results.

All of a sudden Corsinesco's face contorted and turned ghostly pale. He had perceived among the prisoners the very person for whom he had committed the crime, Queen of the Brushes, Le Bigot. That lasted only a moment, but it was enough to reveal how he felt.

Then came the command, "take a knee!" The inmates knelt down, and, simultaneously, the officers of the 113th Infantry gave the order bringing their soldiers to port arms.

Never has the contrast between two groups been greater: the brave, forthright, able-bodied troops on one side and the haggard, parchment yellow faces of the vice laden inmates on the other.

But no one was thinking about that now. All eyes were on the prisoner as he was pushed up to the scaffold by the guards and the aides. Father Boutroy kissed the condemned man twice. Corsinesco shook his head left and right. Monsieur Roch took charge and placed him on the bascule. He had to adjust the lunette to compensate for the large neck of the Italian. That quickly done, the blade was released. The result was a perfect strike.

Just then a cry was heard from among the inmates. It was the Queen of the Brushes who had fainted dead away. He was removed to the prison, and the others followed closely behind.

One last thing, something I had never observed before. Blood from the rapidly beating heart rushed up through the carotid arteries and spurted forth, smoking and streaming above the basket where the body lay.

I didn't have long to examine the scene because the aides went to work, immediately washing blood from the paving stones. The body was placed in a coffin and hauled away to the cemetery at a gallop. Tired and full of emotion, I left the priest saying the final prayers and headed back to the train station for the trip back to Paris.

CHAPTER TENTY-TWO
Patricide: Emmanuel-Modeste Louchard
(18 March 1878)

In the month of March, 1878, a horrible crime was discovered in a small village in the Eure department.[57] A twenty-seven-year-old shepherd named Louchard had hacked his mother to pieces with a scythe specially sharpened for that purpose. Hoping to hide all evidence of the terrible crime forever, he then roasted the head in an oven so that it could not be recognized and placed the remaining parts of the body in a denehole covered with weeds and branches.[58]

A few days later, when the woman's absence had begun to arouse suspicions, a peasant happened by the site. Noticing traces of blood next to the denehole, he deigned to enter the passageway which was forty meters deep. He emerged with a terribly mutilated arm.

Louchard was such a proverbially cruel man that villagers had nicknamed him Louchard the Wicked. It shouldn't be surprising that he was quickly arrested, tried, and sentenced to death despite his persistent denials.

---

[57] The Eure department was formerly part of Normandy. It lies just to the south of Rouen.
[58] Denehole (*marnière*) is usually defined as an ancient hole or shaft of uncertain origin and purpose common to England and northern France.

The condemned man was not otherwise very interesting, but certain particularities of his execution warranted bringing it to the attention of my readers.

The execution was scheduled several times only to be postponed. That served to whet the appetite of the good people of Évreux where the execution was to take place. Each night several hundred spectators gathered at the designated site, an area to the southwest of the city known as Bel-Estat which was used as a training ground by the infantry. It was there in 1859 that a soldier was executed by firing squad. Two years later a child murderer and rapist (like Welker) was executed at the same location.

Finally, it became clear that the execution was about to take place because Monsieur Roch had checked in to the Hôtel du Grand-Cerf at six o'clock in the evening where dinner was waiting for him. Earlier, the executioner had met with the local commissioner, Monsieur Legout, who informed him that the traditional wicker basket would not be necessary because a coffin would be provided by the city. Monsieur Roch objected, explaining the difficulty of making the body fall into such a narrow and squat receptacle such as a coffin. He emphasized the horrible effect that a miscalculation would produce: the condemned man's bleeding trunk would roll on the ground for all to see. However, being that a formal order had been produced, Monsieur Roch had no choice but to comply.

As soon as the public found out about that, the excitement doubled. The word spread quickly and people from miles around were soon on their way to Évreux, the peasants prepared to spend the night at the execution site.

As for Louchard, he remained quite calm. Being of limited intelligence, he remained under the false notion that he could not be executed because he had not confessed. Like so many others, he had counted on the forty-day delay between the sentencing and would-be execution. Since that number had been surpassed, he felt quite relieved.

"I've been saved," he told himself. "Now I can no longer be guillotined. Not only that, I'm going to be pardoned, completely pardoned and set free because I never stopped denying the accusation."

The consoling conclusion, however erroneous, had the effect of doubling his appetite, which was already considerable. At a single sitting he wolfed down as many as six mess tins of soup (the usual amount consumed by two prisoners); and, as though that wasn't enough, with the money his family had given him, he bought other food at the canteen. His voracity amazed everyone in the prison.

At three o'clock in the morning, Monsieur Roch, his son-in-law (Monsieur Berger), and two aides climbed into the execution van and headed for Bel-Estat. Having arrived, they went about the business of erecting the scaffold amidst an ever-increasing and impatient throng that the forces of order had difficulty controlling. From a distance the onlookers could see the death dealing device taking shape and, at its side, the coffin that had caused the disagreement, a barrel-shaped receptacle made from six measures of poplar that had only been roughly sanded. From a distance, I should clarify, because authorities had cordoned off a very large area, and orders were that no one was to penetrate it.

The reporters from the eight well-known newspapers who had been sent to cover the execution (including myself) experienced a great deal of difficulty in their dealings with the public prosecutor, Monsieur Lelu. It was he who issued the order, and contrary to custom, it was meant for absolutely everyone, without exception.

At five o'clock Monsieur Roch began the trek to the prison, some six hundred meters away. Louchard was informed of the impending event, but not to his surprise.

"I knew it," he said.

He had actually spent a dreadful night. Several times Doctor Buisson had to be called to his cell to tend to him because he appeared to be having a stroke. The question is: how did he find out? I can't say for sure, but for the record I can relate the rumor circulating at the time. According to what some were saying, it was the public prosecutor himself who entered Louchard's cell Sunday evening to prepare him for his final hour. That information sent the poor man into a frightful, emotional fit. He had been so convinced that he would be set free that only a quarter of an hour before he had been talking with his guard about his plans for the future and saying how pleased he would be to see his sheep and dog again. Once again, I am only mentioning the matter for the record. I find it difficult to trust the veracity of such a pain-inflicting breach of the law.

Whatever occurred, Louchard had indeed been informed, and it was with a contorted face that he listened to the consoling voice of Father Douin, curate at Saint-Thorin and prison chaplain.

He was offered coffee and brandy, both of which he refused, preferring only to drink a bit of sugar water. He was then turned over to Monsieur Roch who quickly applied the restraints and otherwise prepared the prisoner. The van pulled away just as nearby church bells chimed into the air the joyous notes of the Angelus, which, to my ears, sounded more like a death knell. The van stopped a hundred meters from the scaffold.

A personal note:

The horrible crime of patricide is so revolting to the imagination that the wise statesman Solon of Ancient Greece refused to include it in his proscriptions, believing it impossible. Reality proved otherwise, of course, and the penal codes of various cultures sought to impose the most atrocious penalties to punish it. The ancient Hebrews tied the guilty person in a sack along with a rooster and a viper and threw it into the sea. The Egyptians' solution was impalement by pointed reeds. In other countries offenders were burned alive. In France, in the old days, the criminal's right hand was cut off at the wrist, and then, after having made proper amends, wearing nothing more than a shirt, he was broken alive on the rack, set afire, and his ashes thrown to the wind.

The penal code of 1810 abolished torture. However, for the crime of parricide alone, the amputation of the hand was retained, following which the prisoner was to be taken to the scaffold, barefoot and dressed only in a shirt, where the death decree was read publicly immediately preceding the execution.[59] The penal code of 1832 eliminated the amputation but retained everything else.

Thus, when the doors of the van swung open to allow the condemned man to get out, my colleagues and I were anticipating one of those imposing spectacles that so whet the imagination, especially thanks to the paintings and tales of times gone by. What we saw was quite

---

[59] Grison is quite accurate in his claim. Provision for the amputation is contained in article 13 of the 1810 penal code.

different: a sinister and grotesque Punchinello whose appearance alone would surely provoke universal laughter on any other occasion. Short, rotund and potbellied, with an enormous head supported by a thick neck and shoulders, Louchard was dressed in a pair of black, cotton velour trousers and a matching vest, over which spread a lovely, brand-new, smock of a lustrous blue. Under the vest he wore a short-sleeve shirt with a rounded, priest-like collar that had been carefully ironed. On his head he had wrapped a black crepe cloth that hid two thirds of his beardless face and would have served as a perfect half-mask at a masquerade ball. It is difficult to imagine anything more disgusting than turning this august act of human and divine condemnation into an executioner's carnival.

Those thoughts dissipated rather quickly as my attention was drawn back to the serious situation at hand. Louchard was now inching his way toward the scaffold, dragging his bare feet on the cold wet ground with an aide on each arm. Father Douin showed him the crucifix and, as all chaplains do, tried to keep him from seeing the blade as long as possible. It wasn't the blade he was looking at when he neared the scaffold. It was the coffin.

While his half-mask, his smock, and his vest were being removed, a bailiff dressed in an overcoat, a colored tie, and a round hat, read the death warrant: "As decreed in the judgment rendered by the Criminal Court of the department Eure dated the 28th of January, 1878, etc."

Louchard could not take his eyes off the coffin. He heard nothing, saw nothing other than the box that was wide open and waiting for him. He was fascinated by it.

At the very moment the bailiff read the words "put to death," Monsieur Roch seized the condemned man and placed him on the bascule. There things stopped for a moment. Louchard's neck was so thick and short that it was difficult to find a space between the head and the shoulders to clamp on the lunette. At last the blade fell, as did the head, and the body slid into the coffin.

Now for a rather hideous detail. When the prisoner was placed on the bascule, he was hunched a bit forward. He remained that way until the end, meaning that the body was in a near sitting position when it went into the coffin. That left an enormous, open wound visible above it and four streams of steaming blood spurting high into the air and cascading onto the ground. It was ghastly!

Monsieur Roch and his aides came running. They laid the body out and fit it into the coffin, leaving just enough room to accommodate the severed head. With that finally accomplished, they put the cover on, nailed it down, and placed the coffin on a small cart painted sky blue and pulled by a white horse that set off for the cemetery at a spritely trot.

It was now twelve minutes after six. At long last it was over. For many of the onlookers, even those who had to watch from a goodly distance, it was time, indeed.

Louchard was only twenty-seven years old. Coincidentally, it was the 16th of March, 1877 that he committed the crime. He was executed the 18th of March, 1878. Nearly an anniversary, one might say.

CHAPTER TWENTY-THREE
The Murder on the Rue Poliveau: Discovery of the Crime

The Rue Poliveau murder was a case in which the press proved its worth many times over. From the beginning to the end of the investigation, journalists from various newspapers contributed mightily to the probings of authorities.

Saturday, the 6th of April, 1878, I was in the offices of *Le Figaro* stretched out on a sofa suffering from a bout of neuralgia when word arrived that a discovery similar to the one in the Clichy case had been made on the Rue Poliveau.[60]

Casting aside my discomfort, I leaped into a fiacre and proceeded directly to the address, 42 Rue Poliveau. There, in a room of the Hôtel Jeanson, two human thighs and two arms had been found. The doctor summoned by Police Commissioner Poggi determined that because of their roundness, they appeared to be the limbs of a woman.

The limbs had been brought to the hotel two weeks before by two young men who had rented the room but who had not reappeared. One of them was blond and the other dark-haired. When the dark-haired man rented the room, he gave the following particulars: Gérard Émile,

---

[60] For the Clichy (Billoir) case, see Chapter Thirteen. The Rue Poliveau is located in the Jardin-des-Plantes Quarter of the 5th arrondissement.

twenty-six years of age, a student from Blois. He presented no papers to confirm the information.

The discovery had been made when Monsieur Jeanson opened an armoire in anticipation of renting the room to someone else. He found two bundles, one containing the thighs, the other the arms, both wrapped in gray paper and strips of material torn from a shirt.

The following day, publication of the discovery by *Le Figaro* ignited a firestorm of criticism. I was depicted as a news monger bent on finding crime everywhere. It was obvious to critics that the discovery on the Rue Poliveau was no more than the anatomical leftovers from the medical classes at the Clamart amphitheater located around the corner on the Rue du Fer-à-Moulin. Even the staff doctors themselves were of that opinion. The crime, they were convinced, was not a crime at all. It was a practical joke perpetrated by a medical student.

I persisted, however, believing that a crime had indeed been committed. Looking into the matter further, I had the satisfaction of the consulting doctors Bergeron, Delens, and Brouardel for a second opinion. They pointed out irregularities in the sectioning of the members that were indicative of relative inexperience. Moreover, they said, certain incisions could not have been made by a surgeon's scalpel. That, of course, confirmed for me that it was not a matter of anatomical castoffs, but rather a murder rather like the one for which Billoir was executed.

Additionally, Monsieur Guillot, the investigating magistrate, declared with dogged tenacity that whether it was a crime or a student prank, he was determined to find the two young men who had placed the appendages in the armoire at the Hôtel Jeanson.

Accordingly, he issued the following warrant the 8th of April:

"I, Adolphe Guillot, investigating magistrate of the court of first instance of the Seine, do hereby decree that all law enforcement personnel are ordered to bring before me an individual named or having taken the name Gérard (Émile), a student, supposedly from Blois (Loir-et-Cher), who possesses a firm but heavy writing hand, and who is wanted for murder."

Monsieur Jacob, head of security, wrote the following alert that was delivered to *Le Figaro*:

"Two thighs and two arms belonging to a woman were found in a hotel room, wrapped in black tarred paper, a black petticoat, and three men's cotton, short-sleeve shirts with broad, blue stripes and narrow, pink stripes (Oxford cloth), mended with white cloth, and bearing the initials L. M., the entirety tied together by string and strips of lace.
"One arm has a cauterized injury dressed with an ivy leaf; the hands are wrinkled and calloused.[61]
"As a matter of priority, please instruct your staff to actively investigate the finding, to make known to my office the names of women who have gone missing within the last two weeks, as well as the discovery of any body parts.
"The gendarmerie is requested to publicize this alert throughout the city. Should the victim be identified, that

---

[61] Ivy leaves have long been used for medicinal purposes, ostensibly in this case to reduce swelling.

information will be communicated immediately to the press."

The body parts and their wrappings were made available for viewing at the morgue. As in the Billoir case, false leads began to surface immediately.

There was first of all a pâtissier from Clamecy, Monsieur Guyard, who thought the victim might be his wife. Then there was a certain Monsieur B . . . living on the Rue Stephenson who also thought the victim might be his wife, Florentine, who worked at the Bicêtre hospice. The two claims were quickly found to be erroneous.

While those claims were being investigated, however, Émile Gérard was suddenly arrested. That came about this way. A young, blond woman rented a room at the Hôtel de France et de Hollande on the Rue Bouloi.[62] She registered under the name of Louise Rivers and left, saying that she would return the following day with her luggage. The next day she did return, without her luggage but in the company of a short, full-bearded, well-dressed, man who was introduced as Émile Gérard.

Louise Rivers and Émile Gérard returned again the next day, but were not seen again. Then, on the 14th of April, the woman came back to the hotel. She was arrested immediately. Her name was not Rivers at all, but rather Didier. That same day, in the evening, Émile Gérard was seen wandering about in the quarter. The police were notified immediately. He was accosted from behind by two officers. He turned, lashed out, and took to his heels. His flight was short-lived, however. He was

---

[62] Rue Bouloi is located in the 1st arrondissement not far from the Palais-Royal.

quickly apprehended, arrested, and taken to the prefecture.

There it was discovered that his name was Bernard, not Gérard. When the proprietress of the hotel on the Rue Poliveau was brought in to identify him, she said he was not the man who had rented the room. He was found to be a bellboy living on the Rue Mandar with a young brunette, his legal wife. The poor fellow had assumed the false identity in order to have a good time without getting caught. That ploy had led him straight to the Mazas Prison. He was released, but one can only imagine the scene he faced when returning home.

As bizarre as that episode was, it was soon surpassed by another. Only a few days later, *La Petite Presse* printed a story with the following heading and account:

"Hot on the Trail of the Two Murderers on the Rue Poliveau: Where is the Coachman?"

"Thursday, at twenty to six, a fiacre stopped in front of 39 Rue Poliveau, a wine and tobacco bar located opposite the Hôtel Jeanson and owned by Madame Noël.

"Two individuals got out and went into the tobacco shop. They bought two twenty-five centime cigars.

"Madame Noël noticed how preoccupied the two seemed to be and claimed to have overheard the shorter one say confidentially: 'We bought two cigars here the day we brought the limbs.'

"Then they left in a hurry and jumped into the waiting vehicle.

"One of the two, the shorter one, was properly attired: an overcoat, a black morning coat, brown trousers, and a top hat. He was very dark complected, and he appeared rather nervous and unsettled as he shuffled about.

"The taller one had a large reddish blond mustache, wore a small hat, and was dressed in a heavy, brown overcoat, a type of ulster.

"Madame Noël was so taken aback by what she had heard that she didn't think to try to detain the two miserable wretches. Only as the fiacre was pulling away did she think to inform the police officers who were stationed on the Rue Poliveau in case the criminals returned to the scene of the crime.

"The officers tried to follow but were quickly outdistanced by the horse-drawn vehicle. The prey had gotten away.

"At this late hour as the present column is being written (half past midnight), the coachman must have been found and must have made his declaration to authorities.

"The individuals in question have not yet been arrested, but suspicions are giving way to certainties. The investigative net that has been cast is tightening and it seems likely that by tomorrow the police will have the guilty parties within their grasp. Then, in order not to let anything go amiss, they will proceed slowly and methodically, before swooping down on the culprits and putting an end to this lugubrious drama.

"We are calling on all our readers to inform the prefecture of any and all information pertaining to the events that we have related. The Rue Poliveau is rather out of the way, so to speak, so any coachman taking said individuals to the indicated address would be sure to recall it."

All the while, the two men who had caused the tumult were working away peacefully in their offices. They were, in fact, Messieurs Monréal of *Le Nouveau Journal* and Friedlander of *Le Petit Parisien*. They had gone to visit the crime site and had stopped off to buy cigars at Madame Noël's shop. With regard to Madame Noël's statement, having just discussed the crime at length with the proprietor of the Hôtel Jeanson, one of the reporters said to the other: "And to think they may have come here to buy cigars before dropping off their bundles." The whole ordeal had resulted from a misunderstanding.

Now authorities were hard at work, and the victim's identity was about to be discovered. Here is how that came about.

There was a reporter named Peyrocave working for *La Liberté*. From the South and very dark complected, he was an intense, boisterous type, zealous to the point that he would go to any lengths to track down a story.

Peyrocave was bent on discovering the victim's identity. So he began reviewing recent missing persons reports, a task on which the police were already at work. As luck would have it, he chanced upon the right one first.

Among the women who had disappeared was a milk vendor by the name of Gillet who lived at 8 Rue de Paradis-Poissonnière.[63] Information contained in the report indicated that she had disappeared the 23rd of March, 1878, that is to say about the same time that the

---

[63] The street is located in the 10th arrondissement. Its name was changed to Rue de Paradis in 1881, two years prior to the 1883 publication of *Souvenirs de la Place de la Roquette*.

body parts had been brought to the Hôtel Jeanson. Additionally, one of her compatriots and friends, Madame Grand, who ran a vehicle rental business on the Rue Granges-aux Belles, told the reporter that the missing woman had a cauterized injury on her arm.

That did the trick.

Monsieur and Madame Grand, convinced that the victim was their friend, went to the Rue Paradis-Poissonnière. Having obtained information from Monsieur Leroux, concierge at the residence, they set off for the morgue. When they arrived, they discovered that it was after hours. Not to be deterred, they went directly to see Monsieur Jacob, head of security, and gave him a very detailed description of Madame Gillet. They mentioned the cauterized injury that Madame Grand had helped dress several times. A few years earlier, while working as a shawl finisher, the thumb on Madame Gillet's left hand was crushed and required cauterization.

Monsieur Clément, high judicial commissioner, and Monsieur Guillot, the investigating magistrate, witnessed the couple's depositions. When the severed limbs were shown to Madame Grand, she recognized them, as well as the spot where the cauterization had been applied. She also recognized the petticoat as the one that Madame Gillet usually wore.

Several of the woman's neighbors were of the same opinion. The victim had thus been identified. But one question remained: who killed her?

CHAPTER TWENTY-FOUR
The Murderers

Once the victim had been identified, the investigation took a wrong turn. Evidence had turned up according to which Madame Gillet had been a woman of questionable comportment. Her dalliances were reported to be numerous, and suspicion fell on her various partners.

In 1875 she had taken a lover who was a concierge employed at a Boulevard de Strasbourg address. He was ultimately found to be married and living in Montmartre. She also had relations with a street performer/wrestler whom she had met three years before at the Place du Trône fair grounds and who was known to visit her on several occasions.[64] Another man, a sixty-five-year-old farmer from the Sannois region, also had come calling from time to time.

Madame Baron, a neighbor who read her mail for her–Madame Gillet struggled to read even simple texts–indicated that she had received an invitation to dine in Belleville, 23 Rue Jouye-Rouve, at the residence of a cobbler named Herbelot. Herbelot was arrested, along with another individual, a thirty-five-year-old wine merchant listing no address. Finally, authorities were looking for a certain Monsieur Deruel, a commercial agent

---

[64] The Place du Trône is Paris's modern-day Place de la Nation. The fair itself dates from the tenth century. Early on it attracted acrobats and other such entertainers. It still exists as a seasonal fair (April-May), a festive carnival that attracts millions to its present Bois de Vincennes location.

who, it was said, had sold Madame Gillet a number of securities some time before.

Neither Herbelot nor Robert was recognized by Madame Jeanson as having rented the room at the hotel. As for Deruel, he was quickly determined to be a dead end. But another line of investigation was about to emerge.

It was learned that a few days before her death, Madame Gillet had dealings with a short, dark-complected, young man who was a financial advisor and who had himself disappeared a few days after the murder.

That man, Aimé Barré, had been introduced to Madame Gillet by Madame Seurin, the director of an investment bureau. He lived at 3 Rue Rochebrune, on Parmentier Square, a stone's throw from Monsieur Roch.[65] The police went to the Rue Rochebrune address. Barré was not there. When he arrived, he found Messieurs Guillot and Clément waiting for him. Naturally, he denied having anything to do with the affair, but was taken into custody nevertheless.

Here is his story. Barré had been living in Paris for four years. He was born in Angers and was the only son of a noted wood merchant in that city. When he left Angers, he was in the company of his mistress who had borne him a child, a little girl they left in the care of an elderly woman. Sometime after his arrival in Paris, he was engaged as a fourth-level clerk at the notary practice of Maître Dardevilliers, 14 Rue Thévenot.[66]

---

[65] The Rue Rochebrune is located in the 11th arrondissement. Parmentier Square is today the Square Maurice Gardette.

[66] The Rue Thévenot, in the 2nd arrondissement, was absorbed by the Rue Réaumur.

In that same office was also employed a collection clerk by the name of Demol, a retired gendarme and recipient of the Military Medal, who is presently a concierge at 23 Rue Monge. It was he who was charged with running Barré's errands. Last June, Barré left that practice to accept the position of third-level clerk in the practice of Maître Prudhon on the Rue Gaillon. He remained there only until September, when he received from his father the tidy sum of three thousand francs. He used that money to buy furniture and open an office in an apartment at 61 Rue d'Hauteville, on the third floor, next to the courtyard, for which the rent was eight hundred francs a month. It was the director of the investment bureau, Madame Seurin, who negotiated the lease.

On the 8th of January, for reasons of economy, Barré felt compelled to move from the Rue d'Hauteville address to the more modest Rue Rochebrune address. From the day he abandoned his position as notary clerk, Aimé Barré had been involved in those stock market transactions disparagingly referred to as "jiggery-pokery." During all these coming and goings and changes of address, Barré had not lost contact with the concierge Demol, whom he continued to engage to run his errands.

In the month of October, 1877, Barré charged Monsieur Dubreuil, a Rue Saint-Martin exchange agent, with undertaking a stock market venture in his name. The venture did not pan out, and Barré lost the sum of four hundred francs, for which the exchange agent filed suit against him. Realizing he was about to be litigated, on the 25th of March the former notary clerk had Demol negotiate the sale of three Orleans securities from which Monsieur Dubreuil would retain the four hundred francs in question and return the remaining two hundred twelve francs to Barré.

The 30th of March Demol was sent to collect 3,225 francs from another exchange agent, Monsieur Roussel, 8 Rue Louvois; and finally, the 31st of March, Demol was sent to 16 Rue Thénevot to pay a restaurant bill of four hundred sixteen francs which he had withdrawn from the account at the bank directed by Monsieur Kauffmann on the Rue Dalayrac.

On the night of March 30, after Demol had remitted the sum acquired from Monsieur Roussel, Barré hired a fiacre to take him and Demol to the residence of a friend, a current medical student who lived in the Latin Quarter on an ancient street near the Pantheon. The two had been schoolmates and after coming to Paris had lived together for a while at 35 Rue Grange-aux-Belles. Demol had to wait for twenty minutes outside the door to the apartment.

As they were going down the stairway, Barré explained, "I'm sorry to put you out like that, but my friend had so much work that I had to wait until he could spare a moment. You can't imagine the number of human limbs he brings home to operate on, and what may appear even more surprising, his mistress, who lives with him, doesn't seem to mind."

The 4th of April Demol accompanied Barré to buy a small, wooden trunk called a chapellière, forty to fifty centimeters in height, for which he paid four francs. "It was," Barré said, "to send some clothes to his mistress who had returned to Angers."

Until Sunday, the 24th of March, Barré had been financially stressed, to the point that he had borrowed from Demol one hundred twenty francs in ten- to twenty-franc amounts. On the evening of the 24th, he arrived at Demol's residence, 33 Rue Monge, and gave Demol's wife six twenty franc gold pieces.

All the while the newspapers were full of news concerning the discovery of the body parts and the confirmed identity of the victim. Demol, having followed the reports, suspected his employer and went to the prefecture with his suspicions.

Monsieur Guillot listened closely to his observations and soon shared his viewpoint. He had Barré arrested at his residence on the Rue Rochebrune. As mentioned earlier, Barré denied having anything to do with the murder.

Barré was brought before Madame Jeanson, the hotel owner, but she was unable to identify him. Investigators were not dissuaded, however, and their disposition was about to be validated. Madame Gillet, as I have mentioned, possessed a small fortune in securities, some twenty thousand francs, in fact.

Investigators were able to uncover some of the identification numbers. Monsieur Guillot hastened to put out a confidential circular containing the numbers to all exchange agents. The circular contained the request that he be informed if any information pertaining to them should happen to surface.

The circular produced no results until Demol, having been brought back in for questioning, provided the numbers of the securities he had sold. That's when all doubt disappeared.

Barré was called before the magistrate in his chambers. He could not hide his concern when the judge revealed the evidence that had been gathered against him. He admitted having taken possession of the securities and having sold them, but he insisted that he knew nothing about what had happened to his client or where she might be.

Barré was absolutely adamant and refused to budge from his statement. The following day he was questioned gain. Barré hesitated and appeared more troubled than the day before. All of a sudden he blurted out, "All right, yes, I did it, but I wasn't alone. I had an accomplice."

"Do you want to tell me his name?" Monsieur Guillot asked.

"Yes, yes I do. Since I've had it, I don't want to be the only one. His name is Lebiez."

"And where does he live?"

"In the Latin Quarter."

"Near the Rue Poliveau?"

"Yes, near the Rue Poliveau, Rue des Fosses-Saint-Jacques, in a hotel."

"What is his profession?"

"Laboratory assistant at the Jardin des Plantes."

"Is he a doctor?"

"He is a medical student. He does the dissections."

"Have you assisted him?"

"No."

"But you went with him to the Rue Poliveau? Was it you who registered under the name of Émile Gérard?"

"Yes, it was me."

"Where did you hide Madame Gillet's body?"

"In a trunk."

"The one you had Demol buy?"

"Yes, and we shipped it to Le Mans."

"Why?"

"We expected to go to Le Mans ourselves and get rid of the body."

"To what address did you ship the trunk?"

"The train station."

An hour after the interrogation, which seemed to upset Barré a good bit, Messieurs Jacob and Clément left for Le Mans. At the baggage claim, they were shown a trunk and a crate that had been there for several days. Employees had noticed a rather strong odor coming from one of the two, but they did not pay special attention to it, thinking it was merely something that had spoiled inside. Messieurs Clément and Guillot went about opening the crate, in which they found nothing out of the ordinary. Then they opened the trunk.

After having removed some linens and other items, they discovered a half-decomposed human head resting between two legs that still bore a pair of ladies ankle boots. Beneath the compartment containing those parts they found the torso belonging to poor Madame Gillet. Verifications left no further doubt about the identity of the victim.

A dispatch stating what had been found was immediately sent to Monsieur Guillot. Lebiez was arrested Sunday, the 21st of April at the Hotel des Fosses-Saint-Jacques address given by Barré.

Lebiez was well-liked by his neighbors. After two days the hotel owners still could not believe he could be guilty of such a crime. They changed their minds only after both men had confessed everything.

Here is the sequence of events related to the crime:

Barré was one of Madame Gillet's customers. She brought him milk every morning. While they were chatting one day, Madame Gillet happened to mention that she was momentarily strapped for cash and that she would be interested in selling some of the securities she had accumulated.

Barré, who found himself in a similar financial state, immediately offered to negotiate the transaction in her name. Madame Gillet proved reticent, however, and declined the offer. It was then that Barré conceived the idea of procuring those securities by criminal means.

Barré approached his friend Lebiez with the dastardly idea. It took little cajoling for Lebiez to agree to participate. Two days later, that is to say the 21st of March, Madame Gillet appeared at Barré's door at 61 Rue Hauteville as usual.[67] As soon as the door was closed, the two assassins attacked her, striking her on the back of the head with a hammer.

Madame Gillet fell flat on the tiled floor. Since she was not yet dead, Lebiez picked up a sharp paint scraper and thrust it into her several times. Two of the wounds were inflicted in the area of the heart and proved fatal.

As soon as he determined that Madame Gillet was indeed dead, Barré removed the door key from her body and set off audaciously to retrieve the securities from her lodging. Having found them, he immediately went about having them negotiated at several Paris banks.

With the first phase accomplished, there remained the second phase, the method of disposing of the body. That phase was accomplished by dismembering it surgically, a task they completed over several hours that night and the next day. Then, after having wrapped the victim's arms and thighs in paper and bits of clothing, the

---

[67] It was a short walk from her Rue de Paradis-Poissonnière address. The Rue d'Hauteville intersected the Rue de Paradis-Poissonnière in the 10th arrondissement. According to the public record the murder took place the 23rd of March.

two went to the Hôtel Jeanson on the Rue Poliveau where they abandoned the remains in an armoire, as we know. It wasn't until two days later that they transported the head and trunk to the Montparnasse train station.

On a Monday at two o'clock in the afternoon, Barré and Lebiez were confronted with the dismembered remains at the morgue. Seeing them displayed like that, Barré broke down and confessed again. Up to that point Lebiez had denied any role whatsoever in the crime, claiming his accomplice was entirely responsible. But with the evidence laid out before him, he was moved to confess as well.

By the time they left, however, the two had regained their composure. With a cigarette in his mouth, Lebiez seemed quite relaxed as he climbed into the fiacre waiting to take the men to Mazas prison.

That's not surprising, for Lebiez was a skeptic, or, rather, a cynic. One bit of information proves it beyond a shadow of a doubt. The 12th of April, that is to say only three weeks after the murder, the young man delivered a lecture on Darwinism and the Church before a gathering on the Rue d'Arras. The fact that he was able to do so convincingly reflects a liberated state of mind extremely unusual for someone embroiled in his dreadful circumstances.

Moreover, he had been compelled to appear several times at police headquarters because he was the manager of a radical newspaper that was to appear in a few days, *Père Duchêne*, edited by Hippolyte Buffenoir.[68]

---

[68] The original title, *Père Duchesne* (original spelling), was published by Jacques Hébert during the French Revolution. It

I shall complete my account of the investigation by indicating that the mistresses of both Barré and Lebiez were arrested but found not to have been involved in the crime. As for the rest, the murderers were sentenced to death the 19th of July. Their execution was the last one Monsieur Roch would oversee in Paris.

---

reappeared intermittently at times of political and social stress throughout the nineteenth century.

CHAPTER TWENTY-FIVE
The Execution of Aimé-Thomas Barré and Paul Lebiez (7 September 1878)

The announcement of the execution caused quite a stir in Paris. As I headed to the Place de la Roquette, I wondered what turn of events would make this execution unique.

For the Moreau execution, it was the condemned man's cry of innocence at the point of death; for Billoir's execution it was a combination of pity and sympathy the crowd felt for a courageous, old soldier. For Welker's execution it was the disgust stemming from his cowardice, both in committing the crime and in facing his expiation. For Roux's execution in Versailles, it was the beauty of a springtime sunrise contrasted with the agony of an adolescent. For the execution of Corsinesco in Melun, it was the backdrop of the provincial prison with the condemned man on his knees in the foreground. For Albert's execution it was his haughtiness. For Louchard's execution for patricide, it was the defiance of a brute.

For Barré and Lebiez, it was the element of scandal surrounding their execution that made it unique. The only other execution to rival it in recent memory was the double execution of Frédéric Depré and Joseph Norbert, March 24, 1843, when the scaffold was surrounded by masked revelers returning from a night's glee at the Mid-Lent celebration.[69]

Several newspapers committed the grave error of announcing the exact time and date of the execution of Madame Gillet's murderers. Thrill-seekers rushed to procure a good vantage point from which to view the spectacle. Whatever their calling, they streamed to the Place de la Roquette and fought for spots in the first row: the high-livers of the outer boulevards, the finest Paris has to offer in dancehall girls who plied their trade at the city's gates, the silk-hatted individuals one sees in the evening wandering about the brasseries in the Faubourg-Montmartre.

However, when the reporters arrived carrying their entry permits issued by Monsieur Albert Gigot, the local police chief, the officer commanding the Republican Guard had them met with gun butts.

That deplorable state of affairs lasted until Monsieur Ansart, chief of Municipal police, arrived on the scene. He had the final word in the matter. Having heeded the reporters' claims to right of way, he took the measures necessary to defusing the situation. Soon every one of us was in a position to see.

It was then that I noticed an intelligent modification made to the guillotine. As you will recall, at the double execution of Moreau and Boudas, Boudas blanched and

---

[69] The Mid-Lent ("mi-carême") celebration dates from the medieval period and resembles in character today's Mardi Gras. Depré and Norbert were convicted of murdering a drinking mate for the paltry sum of fourteen francs. Like Barré and Lebiez, they were both young men. The execution took place at the Barrière Saint-Jacques (today the Place Saint-Jacques) in the 14th arrondissement.

shuddered when faced with the aspect of the blade that was stained with Moreau's blood despite repeated washings. In virtually every execution the prisoner's eyes are inevitably drawn to the steel blade gleaming in the early-morning sunshine. As of now a reddish-brown, wooden panel stretching from one upright to the other shields the blade from view.

Another improvement has been inaugurated. Everyone is sensitive to the frightening noise the blade makes at the end of its fall. Now one can hardly hear it. The reason is that the coil springs have been replaced by rubber springs that deaden the sound more completely.

The sun was up now. The appointed hour was nearing. The usual group of Messieurs Baron, Jacob, and Bauquesne, accompanied by the clerk of appeals, Monsieur Barret, had gone into the cellblock and stopped outside cells one and two located opposite each other. Because the two condemned men were to be taken out together, Father Latour, chaplain at La Petite-Roquette next door, had been called in to assist the venerable Father Crozes.

The group went into Barré's cell first. The prisoner had turned in early and was sleeping lightly. The light caused him to open his eyes.

Warden Bauquesne addressed him matter-of-factly: "Aimé-Thomas Barré, your appeal and your plea for mercy have both been denied. May God help you to be strong."

As though he had received an electric shock, a convulsive tremor ran through Barré's body from his head down to his toes. Still disoriented, he said nothing, but rose and began dressing.

Once he had donned his trousers, he asked whether he might have a bit of wine. The brigadier-head guard hastened to bring him a glass. Barré gulped it down. The wine brought the color back to his face.

"Now I'd like to smoke a cigarette, if you don't mind."

He was handed a cigarette freshly rolled. He lit it and began to examine the papers he took from the drawer of the pine table furnished by the prison. He shuffled through them slowly, in order to create the appearance that he was making a selection, but in reality to gain time.

Finally, he made a decision and handed a letter to Monsieur Bauquesne. Then he gave his remaining money to Father Crozes.

"You know who it's for," he said to the priest.

The priest nodded. Barré then asked to spend a few moments alone with Father Crozes. The group assented and crossed over to Lebiez's cell.

Lebiez had played cards until two o'clock in the morning. Then he had read a book on the history of navigation until three o'clock. Overcome by fatigue, he had fallen asleep a scant two hours before.

"Lebiez!" Monsieur Bauquesne called out.

Lebiez did not budge. He had to be shaken in order to wake him from the deep sleep into which he had fallen.

"Ah! Ah! Ah!" came out of his mouth in sharply rising tones. He sat up and looked at the men gathered in his cell.

The warden gave him the same message he had given to Barré. Lebiez leaped from his bed, dressed quickly, and began to go through his papers, as Barré had done.

"Would you like to smoke or have some wine?" he was asked.

"No, thank you."

Spying Father Latour, he gestured for him to come closer. He kissed the priest several times. Then, seeing Father Crozes, who was waiting outside the cell to accompany Barré to the registry, he said to him, "And you, too, my good man." He then kissed him on his two cheeks.

Barré went first, mechanically smoking the cigarette he had to relight twice during his talk with the chaplain. With the formalities completed, he was handed over to Monsieur Roch for the restraints to be applied. "Oh! please don't hurt me," he said, "I promise I won't put up a fight."

In compliance, Monsieur Roch went about his task with great care. Nevertheless, the cord against his skin made the prisoner flinch.

"More wine, more wine!" he cried out.

A glass was brought to his lips. He drank avidly. Then he said, "I'd like another cigarette." But Monsieur Baron made a negative sign.

During Barré's maneuvers to gain time, Lebiez's preparations had been completed. Officials were determined not to prolong his agony. After all, being second in line, he would have to wait while his accomplice underwent the blade.

The procession to the scaffold began. You are doubtlessly familiar with the fateful command "Draw you sabers!" That means that the prison gate is about to open and the condemned prisoner or prisoners will be escorted through.

Barré appeared first. Lebiez followed a few steps behind, his head bowed.

Barré appeared utterly exhausted. Each step toward the scaffold drained him further. Half way there he gave out completely. He would have fallen to the ground had the aides not been grasping him securely. They lugged him to the bascule, and a moment later the blade fell.

Lebiez heard the blade fall. He was stunned by it, but with an iron will he perked up and said in a strained voice, "Let's get on with it!"

Of his own volition, he began walking toward the scaffold. In the meantime the blade had been hoisted into position again. Lebiez walked slowly, slowly enough for me to notice the contrast between his now clean-shaven face and the bearded profile he exhibited at criminal court. Then he picked up the pace and within half a minute found himself standing next to the bascule.

The aides placed their hands on his shoulders. "Adieu, messieurs!" he said in a strained voice.

Just then a voice rang out from one of the windows in the executioners' van: "Bravo, Lebiez!" It was, I was told, a suburban printer and friend of the former manager of the newspaper *Père Duchêne*.

Father Latour stepped away. Lebiez looked down at the bascule now. It was covered with his friend's blood, and he was about to be forced down upon it. His face contracted in disgust.

And the blade fell a second time.

Immediately after the double execution, Father Crozes and Father Latour set off at a gallop in fiacre number 148. The executioners' van, carrying the two bodies to the Ivry cemetery, followed some distance behind. Monsieur Jacob, in his carriage, trailed the doleful procession which was rapidly approaching the Boulevard de l'Hôpital. My colleagues and I were at the rear.

The execution was highly anticipated, as I have stated. All the way along we encountered women who peered out of their windows and signed themselves.

The sun was rising to the left, causing the gendarmes' bandoliers to shine.

At the gate on the road to Choisy, the octroi employees removed their hats. The horse of one of the gendarmes spooked, nearly unseating the rider and coming dangerously close to throwing him into the adjoining wall.

Farther along the route, workers were just arriving at a candle factory. They stopped and stared intently as the green vehicle with small, shuttered windows passed by, a rare sight, indeed.

The caretaker and cemetery gendarme were waiting at the gate. The gendarme had made a special effort to make himself presentable for the occasion.

The two priests were the first to step out of their vehicle. The venerable Father Crozes held in his trembling hands a prayer book and an envelope containing the last wishes of the two men. Procedures had been enacted in order to be certain that the proper body and head were placed together. For the sake of identification, a piece of paper had been inserted into the left pocket of Lebiez's trousers.

The gendarmes followed the priests along a pathway lined with cypresses that flanked the Sisters of Charity section of the cemetery. They all stopped beside a grave that had been dug that morning and which, because of its size, was obviously meant for two bodies.

Two coffins, similar to the ones used in hospitals, had been placed next to the grave. Among those present were the police commissioner of Gentilly, an officer from the 13th arrondissement, and four other police officers.

Down the way the green vehicle, with the small, shuttered windows, waited.

Monsieur Jacob joined the group. He was accompanied by the two guards who had been with the condemned men during their last hours.

The basket containing the bodies and heads of the two men was lifted from the van. The cover was removed. The two bodies were laid out, one backside down, the other on its side.

One of the bodies had a head placed between the knees. It was Lebiez's head. Barré's head, which was covered with blood and sawdust, lay between his feet. Both heads appeared to be sleeping. They were waxen white and completely bloodless. The eyes were wide open. Blood continued to ooze from both trunks. At that moment bells rang out the six o'clock hour. A mere thirty minutes had passed since the execution.

The two bodies were identified officially by Monsieur Jacob and his agents. They then were placed in the coffins. As that was being done, I noticed that Lebiez's trousers were covered with patches and his hands were extremely small.

The chaplains said their final prayers. All hats were removed. At precisely six: ten the coffin containing Lebiez's body was lowered into the grave and covered with the dirt that had been removed. In that dirt we could see a large number of human bones. A jawbone that seemed to be smiling through a grimace sent shivers up and down our spines.

A final request Lebiez made by way of his father was that his body could be disposed of in any manner, but he did not want a mold made of his head. He wanted to disappear forever, he had said.

What a strange contrast: the medical student Lebiez was going to rest eternally in hallowed ground, whereas his accomplice was going to serve as a scientific specimen for doctors. Already, there was a vehicle waiting nearby to take his body away.

Let's follow that vehicle to the medical school and see what we can see.

The body was taken to the demonstration laboratory in the anatomical pathology building of the school. In the absence of Doctor Robin, chair of the histology department, it was Doctor Charcot, professor of anatomical pathology, who had contacted the ministry of public instruction and requested the release of the body.

The empty coffin had been deposited at the entrance to the number seven pavilion. It was a sorry pine box, indeed. The battens, extremely thin as they were, had loosened during the trip. It had been left open, and one could see a pool of coagulated blood at the spot where the neck had rested.

I was shown up to the third floor of the pavilion where I found myself in a vast room furnished with those cold, austere tables that medical science uses to extract from cadavers its elements, its principles, its progress.

The head, which had been separated from the body, was covered with blood. The mouth was closed, the eyes, still wide open, were frightening in that they seemed to be staring at everyone (something I shall never forget).

Among the doctors present, I recognized Messieurs Rochefontaine, Jollyet, Joffroy, Regnard, Labbé, and Bonneville, all of whom were involved in the dissection. Other doctors were conducting experiments with electricity that were being overseen by Doctor Charcot.

Large jars filled with frogs for physiological experiments had been placed on the tables. On the main table was a large and powerful, dual current, electrical apparatus that would be used to conduct contractility experiments on Barré's body and about which I shall have more to say in a while.

When Doctor Charcot and I arrived, the body was already there, having been stretched out on the table to the left as one enters the room. It was still fully clothed and otherwise just as it had been in Monsieur Roch's basket. The clenched hands were still tightly tied together behind the back. It took two aides a full five minutes to untie them. The rope had dug into the flesh, impairing circulation and causing the hands to be limp and colorless. When the rope was loosened, a singular phenomenon occurred: the little blood that remained in the hands suddenly began to circulate and caused them to shake, the one nearly clenching the other as in a final prayer.

Next, the head was washed in order for the resident mold-maker to make the impression. With that process complete, the head was placed on a block and photographed from various angles by the resident photographer, Monsieur Berthier. As he was taking the pictures, I noticed that Barré had jerked his head at the fatal moment, preventing a straight cut and causing the blade to sever part of the chin and shoulder.

The electrical experiments began at eight o'clock. I shall provide specific details for those among you who are specialists and have particular interest in such procedures. The pupils contracted when stimulated directly. That continued until nine: thirty-five when all contractility ceased. General stimulation of the nervous system, however, had no effect on the pupils. Nor did direct stimulation of the spinal cord and the upper and lower parts of the bulb (medulla oblongata).

At ten o'clock the contractility of the ventricles and auricles ceased, even when the electrical current was increased to its maximum strength.

Electrical current was then applied to the following organs: the heart, the spleen, the stomach, the intestines, the bladder, the ureters. No contraction was observed. The same was true for the diaphragm (the muscle that separates the thorax from the abdomen) that was stimulated through certain nerves that are called phrenic nerves. The liver weighed 1,500 grams.

Stimulating the bicep produced a very strong contraction. When the bicep was laid bare and split apart, it produced a lesser contraction. The brachial artery and the median nerve both were found to be insensitive to electrical stimulus.

Barré's teeth were generally rather small, especially the lateral incisors of the upper jaw. Two small molars of the left upper jaw were missing. On the lower jaw the wisdom tooth had not yet emerged from its socket. Now there is pause for reflection!

Examination of the skull revealed a protrusive forehead, very developed parietal and temporal bones, an exceptionally developed occipital bone, and a flattened cranial vault.

Barré's face reflected his unsavory appetites. He was as ugly physically as he was morally. His eyes seemed to ooze crime. His eyelids remained open as normally as in life.

The other organs were then examined. The lungs were healthy and the heart, though perfectly intact, was found to be hardened and resistant to the scalpel. The spleen was normal, the liver offered nothing particular to note. The same was true for the stomach, the pancreas, and the other viscera.

Finally, examination of the brain did not reveal anything worthy of particular attention. That concluded the gross anatomy phase. The microscopic phase was about to begin. Since that aspect is of little interest to readers, I shall turn to other matters.

Everyone reconvened in the amphitheater at five o'clock in the afternoon to go over the results of the procedures that had taken place later in the afternoon.

Barrés's body had been left as it was, lying in the center of that enormous table, the chest cavity still open, the entrails removed, the arms sliced and sectioned, the left leg amputated. Our guide took the severed leg by the foot and deposited it amidst the various organs and bloody shreds. At that point I couldn't help but reflect on the providentially fatal notion that the murderer of Madame Gillet now found himself in exactly the same condition as his victim: dismembered.

I asked to see the head again. Our guide went to look for it. After some time and effort, it was discovered on an upper floor where a practitioner was conducting further experiments on it.[70]

---

[70] As a journalist endeavoring to write a faithful, eyewitness account, Grison limited his descriptions and analyses to those matters and events of which he had direct knowledge. The case of Barré and Lebiez had broader repercussions than that limited perspective reveals, however. Newspaper coverage of the crime, the trial, and the execution extended to England and

CHAPTER TWENTY-SIX
The New Executioner, Monsieur Deibler, and Two Cases of Parricide: Pierre Laprade and Jean Chambe

Monsieur Louis-Antoine-Stanislas Deibler, Monsieur Roch's successor, was born in Dijon in1823. He had just turned sixty when he accepted the position, though he looked younger.

Before cutting off heads, he cut wood. That is to say, he was a cabinetmaker. He first exercised the profession of executioner in 1858. In 1863 he was named chief executioner of Rennes and the five departments of Brittany. He came to Paris in 1871, when a decree prohibited executions in the provinces, and served under Monsieur Roch as adjunct first class.

Not very tall, he appears to be of rather tenuous constitution. He has black hair and a close-cut, horseshoe-shaped beard. He walks slowly and with a slight limp.

---

elsewhere in Europe. Interest was so keen, in fact, that the *New York Times* carried the story in three separate columns. Later, in 1889, Alphonse Daudet would produce a play (*La lutte pour la vie/ The Struggle for Life*) primarily based on Lebiez's interpretation of the Darwinian theory of survival of the fittest, which he used as a lame defense at court. Moreover, the crime itself has made its way into several histories. For a fuller appreciation of the crime and trial as an international phenomenon, see the appendix that follows Grison's text; it includes the official police report (translated) and English-language accounts.

Some twenty years ago, he married the daughter of Monsieur Raseneuf, a harbinger of things to come, for his father-in-law was the chief executioner of Algeria.

The marriage produced two children: a son who is eighteen and works in a novelties shop, a position he will probably leave before long, and a daughter, Clotilde, a lovely eight-year-old brunette who sees the world through large, dark eyes full of surprise. Every morning she bravely sets off for school like an adult, her hands in the pockets of her little cotton dress edged in red.

Monsieur Deibler lives at 3, Rue Vicq-d'Azir, in the 10th arrondissement.

His first execution was rather unfortunate. He had just assumed the position when he was called upon to travel to Agen to oversee the execution of Pierre Laprade.[71]

On the tenth of November, 1878, Laprade shot his mother, his father, and his grandmother. He finished off his father with a sickle. He did the same for the two women by bludgeoning them with his gun butt. He was condemned to death the 6th of March, 1879, and was executed the 19th of May.

I've been told that he put up such a fuss that Monsieur Deibler had to slam his head onto the paving stones in order to gain control of him. I cannot verify that as a fact since I wasn't present and did not see it with my own eyes.

---

[71] That must have been a demanding trip, indeed. Agen is the capital of the Lot-et-Garonne department. It is situated some one hundred thirty kilometers southeast of Bordeaux and over seven hundred kilometers from Paris.

The execution of Jean Chambe for patricide was less moving, but only to a degree. He had strangled his elderly father in order to inherit sooner rather than later the few items of furniture and the few animals he possessed. What was more, he had the audacity to remain shut up with the corpse for over a month. The bed where he slept was quite near the dark cubbyhole into which he had thrust the body.

Chambe was condemned to death the 21st of June. He was executed the 10th of September, eighty days later. He was in such a state of excitation that the prison staff had to administer chloral hydrate several nights in succession.

The execution was held at Saint-Rambert (Loire) the 10th of September, 1879. The prisoner was transported from Montbrison, a two and a half hour trip.[72]

When the blade fell, blood spurted from the trunk and splashed all over the priest's overgarment.

---

[72] Both cities are located east of Lyon.

CHAPTER TWENTY-SEVEN
The Execution of Théotime Prunier (at Beauvais)[73]

It was five o'clock in the morning. The weather was dry but glacially cold. The night was dreary, despite the many stars scintillating in the sky. Pedestrians were streaming forth from all sides and crossing the streets adjoining the Place du Franc-Marché where the execution of Théotime Prunier was to take place.[74]

On the square two thousand people were grouped around the scaffold that Monsieur Deibler and his aides had erected. Several soldiers and a dozen police officers, commanded by Monsieur Pleindoux, held the crowd back. From the outer edge the lanterns of the aides who were coming and going in the middle of the circle resembled so many will-o'-the-wisps on parade.

For the last two weeks, the thrill-seekers had shown up tirelessly at the square in hopes that an execution would take place. They had been anticipating the triple execution of Martin, Hinard, and Prunier. They were now aware that Martin and Hinard had their sentences commuted. All the more reason for not missing Prunier's

---

[73] Beauvais is located seventy-five kilometers to the north of Paris in the Oise department.

[74] Grison's note: Prunier was sentenced to death by the criminal court of the Osie department the 12th of September, 1879 for the rape and murder of a sixty-year-old woman. He threw the body into a river, only to fish it out half an hour later and assault it again.

execution. Therefore, Monsieur Deibler's arrival the evening before with his aides and deathly paraphernalia caused quite a sensation. People had kept vigil all night outside the Hôtel des Trois-Piliers where the executioner was housed. They anxiously awaited the moment when he would make his appearance. In the meantime, until the telegraph office closed, many of them sent messages to friends and family in the outlying area to let them know that at long last the execution was on.

Nearby, on the street bordering the square, a shop window lit up. It was the Café Bataillou that had been making a fortune the last two weeks owing to its proximity to the site. Not only could people go there for sustenance and to warm up, they could also say that they had been to the place where Prosper Martin, one of the men originally sentenced to death, had hatched his crime. He had been in the café at the same time as an elderly man by the name of Barthélemy Toutain. He saw the one hundred forty francs that Toutain was on his way to deposit. Martin rushed out and armed himself with a pitchfork. He waited for the poor old man along the roadway, pounced on him, killed him, and took the money.

The tower clock boldly rang the five: thirty hour. Another bell answered in kind, but more crisply. It was the prison clock, some two hundred meters away. That meant that the condemned man's mass was about to begin.

Prunier knew nothing about the fate that awaited him. The situation of the other two, Martin and Hinard, was rather curious. Each one had been informed by his defense counsel that two of the three had been granted clemency and that he was one of them. But neither knew who the other one was. Therefore, when the three were taken from their cells to the church, all three restrained by straightjackets, Martin and Hinard tried to read the facial expressions of the others in an effort to determine the identity of the one who would not be spared.

The mass was sung by the prison chaplain, Monseigneur Claverie, apostolic protonotary and nephew of Monseigneur Gignoux, formerly the bishop of Beauvais. The present bishop, Monseigneur Hallay, assisted.

At the end of the service, Monsieur Demange, head of prison security, acting in the stead of Monsieur Boisard who was away performing duties in Clermont, went into Prunier's cell.

"You promised you would be strong, Prunier. Now is the time."

"What? It's for today?" Prunier replied calmly.

"Yes. We have to go directly to the registry."

"Okay."

Prunier got up nonchalantly, ready to get on with it. At the registry Prunier met Monseigneur Hallay. The priest offered him several words of encouragement. Prunier bowed reverently. Additionally, the following people were in the registry: the aforementioned Monseigneur Claverie, the clerk of criminal court, Maître Gossin (Prunier's defense counsel), the prison doctor, Monsieur Évrard, two gendarmes and, of course, Monsieur Deibler and his three aides.

Deibler asked for a stool for the condemned man so that he could go about his business. A stool was provided. Prunier's straightjacket was removed, and the clerk read the death decree.

The prisoner's preparation began. It lasted quite a while and was rather painful. Unlike Monsieur Roch, who used the same rope to bind the hands and feet rather loosely, Monsieur Deibler used several pieces of rope of varying thickness and tied them as tightly as he could.

Prunier cried out twice: "You are hurting me! Oh! you are hurting me!"

There was a noticeable difference indeed between Deibler and his predecessor. The one was the living antithesis of the other. Roch was tall and rather corpulent, but very alert, very sprightly, like a Pyrenees mountain goat. Deibler, a Northerner, was small, heavy, lethargic, indecisive–in a word, clumsy.

In the meantime, Prunier complained of having cold feet. His stool was pushed closer to a small stove that was there.

"Thank you very much," he said to Monsieur Demange. "You have always been very good to me. May I shake your hand?"

Monsieur Demange shook his hand, as did the prison guards. Prunier asked to kiss the chaplain. Finally, since the nun in charge of the infirmary had come by, he said to her, "Don't you want to come bid me goodbye?"

The nun approached and offered her hand. Prunier had turned quite pale. Monsieur Demange, sensing some defiance, asked whether he wanted anything.

"Yes, I'd gladly accept a drink."

"Brandy?"

"No, not brandy, rum."

Prunier took the glass of rum and drank it down. Doctor Évrard took his pulse and noted that it was eighty-one pulsations a minute.

The preparations were coming to an end. His collar had just been cut away by an aide. The prison register was given to the executioner. Opposite the name Théotime Prunier, twenty-three years of age, the clerk had written the following:

"Commended to Deibler, Chief Executioner, the 13th of November, at six: fifty-five."

The executioner took the pen and signed his name with some difficulty.

While that was happening, Prunier spoke to his defense attorney, Maître Gossin, who had remained at his side for two months and had moved heaven and earth to save him. "And you, my attorney," he asked, "will you kiss me?"

The young attorney did as he wished. We went down the five or six steps that led from the registry to the prison courtyard where the executioner's van was waiting. As Prunier was about to climb into the vehicle, he asked timidly, "May I have a cigarette?"

Monsieur Demange was hesitant. Maître Gossin took one out, lit it, and passed it to Prunier. The prisoner took four or five puffs and threw it away. "It's not the same now," he said.

The prison gates opened. The large seminary located across the way came into view. As I indicated, The Place Franc-Marché is situated some two hundred meters from the prison. It took a mere three of four minutes to cover that distance by following the Rue Verte and the Rue Neuve-de-la-Prison, before turning onto the road to Calais.

Prunier seemed quite indifferent. While Monseigneur was talking to him, he turned his head to look at the crowd that was grouped around the square. He appeared to be looking for familiar faces.

We were now in the full light of day. Eight men from the 51st Infantry and two brigades from the gendarmerie had herded the crowd into a large circle perhaps fifty meters in diameter. Lieutenant Colonel Edon, first in command, and Monsieur Nonancourt, second in command, were in charge of the armed personnel.

The executioner's vehicle arrived in the center of the circle. The chaplain and the condemned man got out. They stopped a meter from the bascule. Deibler walked up and was about to take hold of the prisoner, but Monseigneur Claverie had not finished. He continued to urge the condemned man to resign himself to his fate. Prunier shuddered and became quite anxious.

That scene went on for a painfully long time. I looked at my watch. One, two, three minutes went by. Never had I witnessed such a long period of time between the arrival of the van and the fall of the blade.

Prunier looked all around. He asked whether the gendarmes who had arrested him were there. He was told they were not.

Yet another minute passed. Sixty seconds became sixty centuries. The group on the scaffold was motionless. Deibler was pale, and that made his horseshoe-shaped beard look all the darker. The chaplain, an ascetic figure, was pale as well. Prunier alone had retained his color.

Ah, finely! The priest kissed the prisoner. He held out the crucifix, and, placing his hand on his forehead, blessed him. Prunier was now in the hands of the executioner. Far from throwing him precipitously, brutally, onto the bascule–which was for Monsieur Roch an act of kindness, Monsieur Deibler eased him down slowly and, just as slowly, released the blade.

Prunier's head had finally fallen. It was a few minutes after seven o'clock.

The body and the head were placed together in the basket and taken to the cemetery. Several doctors were waiting for it there: Messieurs Évrard and Lesage (both from Beauvais), Chevallier and Lesguillon (both from Compiègne), Rochu (from Neuilly-en-Thelle), and Decaisne (a member of the Institute in Paris). It was Monsieur Évrard who had applied for and received permission to take charge of the body. He also was responsible for putting together the team of doctors that would perform the experiments.

I followed the experiments with particular interest, for, beyond their inherent scientific value, they were also relative to a controversial question: Does life subsist after decapitation?

The head had been separated from the trunk for five minutes when it was placed on a stone table, outside, in front of the small, cemetery chapel. Even though the severing had resulted in relatively little loss of blood, droplets continued to pearl at the carotids.

Although the neck was rather short, I could see that the sectioning had been quite clean. The blade had passed between the lower jaw and the chin, the latter of which remained clinging to the neck.

Now I have to tell you that, pinched, stuck with needles, subjected to all sorts of the most painful experiments imaginable, the head did not move, the face remained absolutely impassive, not one muscle reacted in any way. The flame of a candle was placed under the left ear without producing an iota of sensitivity.

Then the skin covering the cranium was quartered. With a scalpel and a saw, the upper portion of the cranial cavity was removed and the brain was taken out. That took at least ten minutes. When the rest of the head underwent electric shocks, neural contractions were produced. The teeth chattered, the mouth remained closed. The eye and the cheek grimaced slightly, the sort of reaction that occurs when a sleeping person is tickled by a feather.

The results were the same for the body. Intact, it was insensitive. The body cavity was opened, the ribs were severed, the heart, liver, and lungs were removed. Application of an electrical current to the arms and legs produced spasms. Doctor Évrard asked me the time: forty minutes had passed since the decapitation.

The experiments were drawing to a close. Application of an electrical current to a shred of skin that had been left hanging from another experiment caused it to rise up, oscillate, and reattach itself violently to the place where it had been originally.

The conclusion the doctors reached, then, was that the movements caused by the application of electrical currents to the body of a guillotined person were completely mechanical and did not demonstrate in any way subsistent life or feeling. The results of this experimentation will be the subject of a paper Doctor Évrard will present before members of the Academy of Medicine and which will demonstrate that death by decapitation is instantaneous.

The autopsy produced the following results: the heart was soft, fatty, and still full of the air aspirated at the moment the blade fell. The brain was quite voluminous. It was found to have adhesions clinging to the surrounding meninges, a condition certainly due to alcoholism.

Prunier had told his attorney, "I must have been terribly drunk to do that." And he admitted as much to Doctor Évrard. "For some time I had been drinking brandy and absinthe," he said. "That day I had drunk a lot and I told myself that there were no two ways about it. I had to get laid."

Was the man who was guillotined a mentally debilitated alcoholic, whereas other criminals had been spared even though they were perfectly sane?

At nine o'clock, Prunier's bloody and butchered body was haphazardly thrown into a grave in the criminal section of the cemetery–without a coffin, without a flower.

I was then aware of a disparity one usually expects to find only in a novel. While in this cemetery eight or ten people examined parcels of human flesh spread out on a tombstone transformed into a surgeon's table, the sun shone above them brilliantly, joyfully, and the happy little birds nestled in the trees above them sang their hearts out.

CHAPTER TWENTY-EIGHT
Police Officer Victor Prévost
(The Murder of Alexandre Lenoble)

At eight: thirty in the evening of Wednesday the 10th of September, 1879, Madame Thierry, living at 153 Rue de la Chapelle, was seated on a bench opposite her house. Looking across the way, she saw a man dressed in a blue coat, gray trousers, and a silk hat carrying a rather large package from which pieces of meat fell onto the roadway. The man approached a sewer drain and dropped something down it resembling a leg of lamb. The woman, suspicious of the man's comings and goings, called a neighbor lady over, and then went to inform the police. The individual in question was able to escape, however, by heading toward the fortifications and disappearing into the freight station.

The police searched the sewer system for the objects. They were quite surprised to find human debris, including an arm. The evidence was taken to police headquarters where Commissioner Lefébure ordered a complete search of the sewer lines of the Rue de la Chapelle and the Rue d'Aubervilliers.[75] The order was carried out that very night. Monsieur Caubet, chief of Paris Police, was informed of the lugubrious matter by telegram and immediately dispatched the head of security, Monsieur Macé, to the scene.

---

[75] The two streets run roughly parallel to each other in the 18th arrondissement stretching as far north as today's Boulevard Périphérique.

Thanks to the thoroughness of the search, police were able to find a hand near a sewer drain of the rue Pajol. The hand was immediately transported to the station on the Rue de l'Évangile. Monsieur Lefébure ordered the search to widen and was met with success. Other parts of the body were found in the sewer line below the Rue Pré-Maudit. However, the head had not yet been found, so it was impossible to identify the victim.

Madame Thierry was summoned to headquarters the following morning. She had been thinking all night about the deplorable scene she had witnessed. The more she thought about it, the more she believed she recognized the man, one of her former neighbors, a policeman.

She first thought that to be inconceivable, but, wishing to have a clear conscience, at headquarters she told Monsieur Lefébure the following:

"Some time ago I used to live on the Rue des Rosiers (today the Rue des roses in the La Chapelle Quarter).[76] Living next to me was a very tall and heavy policeman who, out of uniform, looked very much like the man I saw yesterday."

That was an important clue, for assigned to the Évangile station, whose territory included the Rue des Roses and the Rue du Gué, was a tall and extremely corpulent officer named Prévost who had served as a cavalier guard under Napoleon III. Coincidentally, he should have been on duty from five o'clock to nine o'clock that evening, but he had switched hours with another officer, saying that he had an engagement. Therefore, at the time the murderer was disposing of the body parts, Prévost was off duty.

---

[76] The name change occurred in 1867.

The order went out to bring Prévost in. He was found at the dormitory station for reservists. Interestingly, he was just in the process of talking about the crime and saying that the perpetrator had taken such precautions that he would never be found.

Prévost was taken to headquarters. There, even though he was in uniform, Madame Thierry identified him.

Monsieur Lefébure asked him where he was the night before and why he had switched assignments. He answered that he was tired and had gone to bed.

"Well," Monsieur Lefébure said, "since someone claims to have seen you, we'll just have to go to your residence to verify your whereabouts."

Upon hearing that, Prévost broke down and confessed.

Monsieur Bresselles, the investigating magistrate, and Monsieur Clément, the high judicial commissioner, were called in. They were informed of Prévost's confession and immediately went to his residence on the Rue Riquet.

His lodgings were small but nice, and kept with the meticulous hand of a former soldier. On the right there was a mahogany bed. Opposite it, near a window, there was a sideboard whose shelves were adorned with curios. A small table was situated next to the toilet. The fireplace on the left was adorned with an oilcloth screen. Everywhere on the walls were engravings and photographs of family and friends. A carbine and a dagger were hung together as an ornamental arrangement. Nothing was out of place, nothing that would point to the crime of the night before.

"Where are the other remains," the investigating magistrate asked.

"I threw them into sewer drains and cesspools all over the place."

What he said was true. Police had spent the morning checking cesspools in the quarter. They found bare bones, pieces of flesh, and strips of skin. On a table in the morgue doctors reassembled the body parts. There were seventy items in all. Only the head was missing.

"And the head?" the magistrate asked again.

The officer pointed to the fireplace. The head was indeed there. It belonged to a slim, mustachioed man with thin, dark brown hair who was perhaps forty years of age. Nearly bloodless, the head looked like those wax models one sees on the shelves of beauty salons. The hair and mustache were quite curly. The face itself was of a pronounced regularity. The mouth was half open and the lips slightly pursed. The teeth were white and well formed. The eyes were gapingly open with what one would believe to be fright. In the back of the head there was a triangular hole some six centimeters wide. The skull was completely caved in. Blood had flowed onto the hair on the back of the head.

Prévost was asked the name of the victim. Here is what he said:

"Two weeks ago a jewelry peddler named Lenoble appeared at my door and offered for sale a watch and a chain payable in installments. I told him that I had no need of such items. The man left, but said he would return in a few days. He returned on a Saturday and showed me a medallion that interested me. We were to conclude the deal the following Wednesday.

"Yesterday, which was Wednesday, I was to work the evening shift, so I was free until then. I went out for breakfast. When I came back, the concierge said Monsieur Lenoble had come by earlier and would return in a little while. I waited for him. It was a little after twelve o'clock when he arrived.

"He spread out before me a variety of jewels from his cases, and, after having given me the medallion I had chosen, he was in the process of making out the forms for the sale and payments.

"Then, stunned by the valuable items spread out before me, I leaned over and opened my trunk. I took out a heavy iron ball and smashed it against the back of Lenoble's head.

"The man fell dead at my feet. I cut off his head with my saber-bayonet and proceeded to cut up the body as best as I could."

"Wasn't there a lot of blood?" Monsieur Clément asked.

"Very little. At about five o'clock I went down to the courtyard and fetched a bucket of water. After I had placed all the body parts in a basket, I washed the floor with the assistance of a broom."

Prévost showed the magistrate the spot where he had put the broom. The bristles had been freshly cleaned. When questioned about the other locations where he disposed of the body parts, he indicated the Rue d'Aubervilliers and the Poissonniers postern, beyond the rampart, where police found the bladder and part of the entrails. As the questioning was ending, he said he intended to boil the head in order to disfigure it completely.

Prévost was first transported from the Rue Riquet to the police station on the Rue de l'Évangile and then to the prefecture where he was incarcerated. For their part, investigators spoke at length with the other renters on the Rue Riquet. No unusual noise was heard by any of them.

Prévost's story was confirmed by the concierge. The morning of the crime he had gone out in uniform with a newspaper in hand at approximately seven o'clock. One of his neighbors, Monsieur Thomas, met him on the way and said, "There has been a nasty occurrence in our quarter. Human remains have been found on the Rue Pajol."

Prévost replied, "I'm sure my colleagues will inform me."

The concierge provided important insights into Prévost's behavior. He had several mistresses. He favored one in particular, a former chamber maid and present ironer who worked in the La Chapelle Quarter. She had visited him several times in his quarters.

The arrest sent personnel at the prefecture into a tizzy. Prévost was seen as an ideal policeman. Since his hiring he had never been reprimanded for anything. His colleagues found him to be most trustworthy. After his arrest, however, they came to some disturbing realizations. Prévost loved to talk about crimes involving dismemberment. He joked about them all the time.

On day, during a conversation with a fellow officer about a potential altercation, he had said, "I'd just cut him to pieces, I'd debone him."

He also said in a conversation concerning the Billoir trial, "If it were me, I wouldn't get caught. If I decided to kill someone, I'd do him in and then I'd cut off his nose and his ears. I'd skin him like a calf. I'd gouge his eyes out. I'd cut him up into tiny pieces and scatter them over a large area. Out of sight, out of mind."

Another officer who had worked with him quoted him as having said: "Bah! When you cut up an animal or a man, what's the big deal? When they're dead, they're dead. That's the way to get away with murder!"

A similar statement was also attributed to him. "It's a piece of cake to cut off a man's noggin. It's really a sweet operation."

Prévost's colleagues took all that as being nothing more than rather bad humor. They didn't think for one moment that their model officer was serious.

As for the victim, Alexandre Lenoble was a nice fellow who had been an employee for three years in Monsieur Roullon's jewelry shop at 23 Rue Saint-Sébastien. He had left that position only two months before to accept employment with Monsieur Secrétin, 2 Faubourg du Temple. He was forty years of age and had been married for several years. During the day his two children were kept by his maternal grandmother who lived at 3 Boulevard des Filles-du-Calvaire. His wife was thirty years old and worked as the first linen maid at the Café Riche.

As one can see, it was a model family.

CHAPTER TWENTY-NINE
The Murder of Adèle Blondin

Even though authorities had discovered that Prévost had dismembered, deboned, and skinned the body with uncanny skill and that he had just as skillfully disposed of the seventy-eight pieces of remains, they were still not completely satisfied. They were still faced with the mystery of his prior activities. A woman, his mistress, had disappeared several years before. Prévost had been questioned at the time, but since there seemed to be no motive, his account of the matter appeared to be completely in good faith. He explained that his mistress had left him and that he had not seen or heard from her since. So that aspect of the investigation was closed.

But once it was known what to expect from him, that he was indeed capable of murder, the investigation into the strange disappearance of Adèle Blondin was reopened. Investigators pressed him hard for answers. Finally, he confessed to that crime as well. This is what they learned:

Adèle Blondin, Prévost's mistress, died in exactly the same manner as Lenoble. Sewer drains were used to swallow up the remains. One sole vestige remained: the head. At that time in the La Chapelle Quarter, excavation of an embankment of the fortified wall was underway.

It was there that Prévost disposed of the head. He agreed to take officials to the spot and to oversee the retrieval. Following his instructions, workers began digging in a ditch. Just as Prévost had indicated, they found his mistress's head there. It had been buried for four years.

Adèle had been for many years the housekeeper/caretaker of an elderly man whose generosity had made her rich. When he died, she had amassed some thirty thousand francs. She had a poverty-stricken sister whom she helped out from time to time. Otherwise frugal to a fault, the only extravagance she allowed herself was her unflinching taste for fine food.

A lengthy period of careful premeditation prepared the way for Adèle Blondin's death. Tired of the low rate of 1,500 francs per year that her state investments earned, she planned to invest her money privately. That plan was put into operation toward the end of 1875. As a consequence, she realized a profit of several thousand francs.

Prévost was apprised of the windfall. He had debts. He needed another source of income. His deviousness went into action. He was quite aware of his mistress's habits. She usually carried on her person her investment certificates and her favorite jewels. So he invited her to his apartment where, on the 27th of February, 1876, they would enjoy a sumptuous Sunday dinner together.

Adèle arrived at noon. The table was set. The dinner was ready. Prévost waited until dessert to kill her. He then cut up the body, using a knife to slice into the flesh and a saw to cut through the muscles. In the course of the operation, blood stained the wooden bedframe. Undaunted, in perfect control, Prévost treated the stains with ink. He had already worked out a plan to dispose of the body. He also knew exactly what he would do with the money from the theft. Up until that time he had been renting furnished quarters. He had decided to buy furniture, to move elsewhere, and to live more lavishly.

The 3rd of December, 1879, Prévost appeared before the criminal court of the Seine. He was sentenced to death. His execution was carried out the 19th of January, 1880.

CHAPTER THIRTY
The Execution of Victor Prévost

How would Prévost conduct himself? Would he be brave or cowardly? Would he walk adroitly to the scaffold or would he have to be carried? Those were the questions people were asking for two weeks prior to the execution.

For most people who had followed the case closely since the trial, there was little doubt. He had collapsed, trembling and as pale as a ghost at criminal court; his days and nights in his cell had been smitten with hideous visions that led to frantic tears and outbursts bordering on insanity. They felt that, when the time came, the executioner would find nothing more than an inert and speechless man, virtually dead already. Others felt that, in the end, he would face up to his crimes and would go to his death courageously, like Billoir, a former soldier, as was he.

In any event, people were quite excited about the prospect of his execution and anxiously awaited the fatal day. That is why, when a Monday was selected for the execution, a rarity, a larger crowd than expected turned up.[77]

Of course it was no picnic to brave the elements for three to four hours at the Place de la Roquette when

---

[77] Mondays have always been problematic in Western culture. In France, especially, weekends of heavy eating and drinking had made Monday absenteeism a problem even before the industrial revolution.

temperatures dropped to minus six degrees Celsius. The numbing wind blowing unimpeded from the Place Voltaire to Père-Lachaise cemetery caused onlookers' eyes to tear. The mounds of resplendent snow that had been piled on each side of the square added humidity to frigidity and chilled them to the bone. Minutes seemed like hours in the lugubrious darkness punctuated only by the red glow of lanterns while the executioners' aides went about erecting the guillotine. A mournful silence reigned, interrupted from time to time by the footsteps of police officers taking position and shivering in the hooded coats that made them look like ghosts.

As usual, the square was policed by the brigade from the 11th arrondissement, commanded by Monsieur Siadous. The perimeters were patrolled by the 20th (Monsieur Gallot) and the 12th (Monsieur Brocheton). Two central brigades, commanded by Messieurs Barraz and Jarrige, served as backups and were assisted by a company of municipal guards on foot and a peloton of mounted guards. Orders had been issued that morning to prevent anyone from gaining access to the area immediately surrounding the scaffold. Instead of the usual cordon of police officers spaced out in single file along the sidewalk, officers and guards three abreast sealed off the area.

Even the press corps had to wait beyond that ironclad circle. As a distraction, in order to break the monotony, we watched the latecomers, snuggly attired in their coats and mufflers, who flitted about hoping to find someone they knew to make room for them. Then, one after the other, officials appeared on the scene: Monsieur Caubet, chief of the Paris police, Monsieur Macé, head of security, and, of course, Father Crozes in his faithful fiacre number 148.

There was an interesting incident. A prison transport vehicle came and parked opposite the scaffold. It had come to take a number of young Petite-Roquette inmates to the Lyon railway station. A condemned military man escorted by a dozen guards was also taken on board. That ate up some time. From time to time each of us trotted up and down in an effort to keep warm.

At six: thirty troops from the gendarmerie made their entry, hats cocked, and took their position opposite the scaffold along the Rue de la Roquette. We all knew what that meant. The prologue had come to an end. It was time for the tragic drama to begin.

Several of us approached Monsieur Caubet to ask whether he might be able to find a place for us to view the execution. The chief of Paris police was extremely gracious. Officer Berraz was more than obliging when undertaking the difficult task of squeezing twenty of us in amongst a group that was already tightly packed. Since I had been inserted between two police officers, I asked them their opinion of Prévost's execution.

One of them did not hesitate. "It would have been a terrible shame if his sentence had been commuted. He soiled the uniform and it needs to be cleansed. If it takes all his blood to do it, so be it!"

It was now six: forty-five. The guillotine had been ready for some time. The blade had already been tested and proved in good working order. The rope used to hoist it was removed from the pulley. It was time to go into the prison. Police commissioner Baron signaled to Monsieur Macé to join him.

Monsieur Macé was somewhat pale. It was his first time to witness an execution. That is not to say that he had not shown courage in the line of duty. He certainly had during the fire on the Rue Albouy, at the Estracade de Saint-Louis the day of the Vincenzini murder, and on other occasions.[78] It goes to show that even a veteran such as he is not beyond being nervous about an execution. Nevertheless, he summoned his usual self-mastery and marched off with Monsieur Baron to the prison where they were awaited by Warden Bauquesne. Together they went to Prévost's cell.

The prisoner was wide awake. Did he suspect something? In any event he had become resolved. As much as he had doubted, as much as he had hoped against all hope for a reprieve, animal instinct had finally won out over the throes of mind. It had become a case of matter over mind.

In an absolutely calm voice, he asked, "Is it for this morning?"

Monsieur Bauquesne nodded his head and told him that all efforts to the contrary had failed and that it was a time for courage.

"Don't worry," the prisoner replied. "I'll be strong."

Prévost was a mere shadow of himself. Any of his former colleagues who saw him would surely not recognize him. He was no longer the proud, former soldier or the model police officer who won so many hearts. He was no longer the fresh and healthy man I saw at crimi-

---

[78] A major fire on the Rue Albouy occurred the 7th of October, 1863. It left three people dead, including a police officer, and many injured. The loss was estimated at a million francs. The Estracade de Saint-Louis was an ancient bridge upstream from the Île Saint-Louis. In February of 1871, during the Commune, police officer Vincenzini was assigned to plain-clothes reconnaissance duty involving a demonstration. He was recognized as a policeman, bound to a plank, thrown into the water, and stoned to death. The bridge was demolished in 1932.

nal court. He was not even the condemned man with the withered and spotted face who had been transferred from the Conciergerie to La Roquette. He had become a tall, emaciated skeleton of a man. His cheeks were sunken, his cheekbones protrusive. The absence of a mustache made his nose appear hooked. His forehead was yellow and furrowed. His entire skin had a cadaver-like hue about it that none of us had ever seen before, not even on Welker, the infamous murderer of the Rue Nationale.

For all that, he was as calm as could be. He got up to get dressed and asked whether he could change into more presentable clothing. He was told it was of no use. He asked whether he might wear his slippers because his shoes hurt him.

Father Crozes walked over to him. Prévost accepted graciously his words of comfort and handed him a small package for his brother.

The prisoner's hair and beard were cut expeditiously. The other preparations were quickly concluded as well.

Monsieur Deibler followed protocol and asked, "Is this the condemned man?" Having received the affirmative reply, he continued, "So be it."

It was nearly seven o'clock, but the sun had not yet risen. Father Crozes read the prayers for the dying. Prévost listened intently and murmured, "I do hope my colleagues will forgive me for the way I have compromised our wonderful profession."

When he was asked whether there was anything else he wished to confess, he responded, "I have confessed to the two crimes I committed. That's more than enough, unfortunately. But that's the extent of my crimes."

Dawn finally broke. The register was signed. The prisoner was led away.

Outside came the command: "Draw saber!"

Everyone being familiar with the command, all eyes turned toward the prison gate that was already swinging open. The light was so dim, however, that all I could distinguish was a group of men coming toward us. As they neared in the half-light, I was able to make out Prévost who was a head taller than the others.

"He seems okay," someone closer than I observed.

Finally I could see for myself that he did seem all right. He walked adroitly, steadily, toward the guillotine, towering above Father Crozes who only came up to his chest. Next to the bascule, he bent down and gave Father Crozes a resounding kiss on each of his cheeks. Then he kissed the crucifix.

"Be strong, my son," the chaplain said.

"Don't worry. I will."

Those were his last words. Deibler placed his hand on his shoulder. He maneuvered him onto the bascule rather quickly and released the blade.

The outstretched and rigid body slid into the basket. It was soon joined by the head. Together they were lifted into the funeral van which jerked away and headed for the Ivry cemetery.

We reporters jumped into a waiting vehicle and followed the cortege. Our course took us along the Rue de la Roquette, the Place de la Bastille, the Rue Contrescarpe, the Austerlitz Bridge, and the Boulevard de l'Hôpital. Street sweepers and workers on their way to their jobs stopped to watch the cortege go by. A gendarme with saber in hand led the way. In front of the funeral van rode three gendarmes, one on the left and two on the right. Behind followed Father Crozes's fiacre, Monsieur Macé's vehicle , and two vehicles filled with reporters. The whole moved swiftly along at a fast trot. Death moves quickly in such circumstances. It took a mere forty-five minutes to reach the cemetery, and it's a fair distance.

Whether it was the Avenue d'Italie, the road to Choisy, or the city gate, people had got wind of this cavalcade and came to their windows to see for themselves. We arrived at the cemetery. The cortege disappeared inside. At a distance of some two hundred meters a group of men were waiting: Monsieur Kuehn, police commissioner of Gentilly, Monsieur Provendier, police officer from the 13th arrondissement, and the gravediggers.

The grave had already been dug: a square hole equidistant in depth, length, and width. A pine coffin fashioned from wood no thicker than a sheet of cardboard had been placed next to it.

The body was already rigid, even though we had arrived at seven: forty-five, exactly on time, as everyone recognized. The head was then removed from the basket, a waxen head if ever there was one. It was placed in the coffin between the dead man's legs. The mouth had contracted into a rictus and seemed to be kissing the right thigh.

Father Crozes recited the final prayers. A saint in his last days, there he was, the poor man, bareheaded and chilled to the bone by the cold, moist wind. He was shivering, but he prayed fervently. At long last he finished. Monsieur Macé helped him into the fiacre. The coffin was nailed shut (two nails, no more) and was lifted into the hospital vehicle. Its destination was the clinic at 15 Rue de L'École-de-Médecine. The School had requisitioned the body.

At the cemetery the moisture spotted with blood was wiped from the basket. There had actually been very little blood. Prévost had become a skeleton of a man.

Doctor Robin, who had requested the cadaver, was not present at the medical school. Whatever the misunderstanding that led to his absence, it surely compromised the value of any experimentation. It was already eight: thirty, an hour and a half since Prévost's death, and the body was already cold. It was going to be difficult to discern any sensitivity at all.

So the experiments had to be limited to a simple autopsy. The body was opened and doctors removed the heart, the liver, the spleen, the intestines, the eyes, and the brain. These they placed in a variety of jars to be studied at their leisure. The rest of the body was dissected into small parts, ironically, just as Prévost himself had done with his victims.

CHAPTER THIRTY-ONE
Louis Ménesclou
(The Crime)

Billoir's crime was hideous. Prévost's crimes were more hideous still. But for abject horror, it was Louis Ménesclou's lot, at the tender age of twenty, to outdo the both of them. It was a case that inflamed all Paris.

At number 155 Rue de Grenelle, on the ground floor, lived the Deu family, nine in all, including seven children.[79] Thursday, the 15th of April, 1880, at three o'clock in the afternoon, Madame Deu went to visit her husband at Necker Hospital where he was being treated for pleurisy. The children remained at home.

A rainstorm that descended on Paris forced the children to abandon their play in the courtyard. Little four-year-old Louise told her sister that she wanted to go upstairs to the sixth floor (where Ménesclou lived) to ask her little Friend Victorine for the doll she had promised her. Her sister accompanied her upstairs. They knocked on the door of the apartment where Victorine lived with her parents. No one was home. Louise sat down on a stair step and insisted on remaining there until the family returned.

"I want my doll!" she said.

---

[79] The number 155 Rue de Grenelle is located west of the Champ-de-Mars, between the Rue Duvivier and the Rue Ernest Psichari in the Gros-Caillou Quarter of the 7th arrondissement.

There was no reason for concern. Louise was in the habit of wandering around on other floors. People found her so adorable. Affectionately, she was called Louisette. She was so nice that everyone spoiled her. So, initially, her absence was no cause for alarm. But after more than an hour had gone by, the mother, who had just returned from the hospital, began to worry.

"Zézette!" she called up the stairs.

No answer. She climbed the stairs and knocked on the door. No one answered. Then she went back down and shared her concern with Madame Touré, a laundress who lived across the hall.

"I hope that brat of a kid upstairs hasn't killed my child," she remarked.

That turned out to be an unwitting premonition.

The misfit upstairs was reason for concern. The twenty-year-old had been nothing but trouble for his family. For that reason he had been sent off to become a ship's apprentice. When that didn't work out, his parents tried in vain to find work for him. Taking advantage of his weak-willed mother, a weakness for which she has since been punished, he spent his days frequenting the cabarets near the École Militaire–a vice-ridden area, it is well known. He came home only to eat, drink, and sleep. The neighbors all saw him as nothing more than a carouser, capable of anything but good for nothing, and potentially dangerous.

One can certainly understand Madame Deu's apprehension when she heard that her daughter had gone upstairs and had not returned. Beside herself with fear, she knocked on Ménesclou's door. At first no one answered. Another of her daughters told her, however, that she knew the young fellow was there. So she continued to knock. Louis Ménesclou opened the door.

"Have you seen my daughter?" she asked. "I have an idea she's inside."

"What makes you think she's here? What do you think I'd be doing with her?"

The poor woman went back downstairs. Her suspicions were growing by the minute. She ran as quickly as she could to the commissariat on the Avenue de Lamothe-Picquet. She was greeted by an employee who did not take her complaint very seriously. In that quarter children flitted about from morning to night. An absence of few hours was of little concern.

Madame Deu returned home her eyes full of tears. She went back up to the Ménesclou apartment. The parents were home now. Madame Deu accompanied them into the son's bedroom where the young man was sleeping. He was asked again whether he had lured the child into the apartment. He again denied having done so, then rolled over and turned his face to the wall. Nothing was found under his bed other than an old crate.

Now at that very moment the wretch was lying on top of poor Louisette's body. He had hidden it beneath his mattress. And he spent the night that way.

The next day, Madame Deu, who hadn't slept a wink that night, contacted a chimneysweep on the Rue Cler. She asked him to check the roof and to look about the attic. The chimneysweep climbed up to the roof and smelled a nauseating odor.

"It's flesh that someone is burning," he told himself, and he came back down and informed some of the renters. Some of them went directly to see Commissioner Bugnottet. He was not there. But Monsieur Véron, his secretary acting in his stead, agreed to look into the matter.

When he arrived on the landing, it was obvious that the odor was coming from Louis Ménesclou's apartment. The door was quickly knocked down. An appalling spectacle awaited him.

Louis Ménesclou, dressed in his naval trousers, a blue-striped shirt, and rope-soled sandals, was washing his hands. The floor and furniture were drowning in blood. On the dining room table were scattered hunks of bleeding flesh. From the mixture of flesh and bones emerged the two feet of a child, still clad with their small shoes.

A bucket half full of water reddened by blood had been placed at the foot of the table. In one corner of the room, next to a parcel of blood-stained cloths, lay a cleaver to which bits of bone and shreds of flesh were clinging. Heavy, nauseating smoke was coming from the open door of an oven. Inside the half-charred head of a child was clearly visible.

Louis Ménesclou was taken, or rather, dragged to the police station. There he was searched. In his pants pockets police found two little arms, severed at the elbow, with their darling, little, plump hands intact. When the police arrived at his door, Louis Ménesclou, in a moment of madness, had tried to hide those parts of little Louise's body.

Officers had to restrain themselves to keep from killing the monster on the spot.

"It was you who killed the little girl from downstairs?" Monsieur Véron inquired.

"Yes."

"Why?"

"I don't know."

"How did she end up in your apartment?"

"I called to her during the storm, in order to give her some lilacs. But she screamed."

"Then what did you do?"

"I strangled her."

"Why?"

"Because she was screaming."

"Why was she screaming?"

No response.

Ménesclou admitted cutting his victim into thirty-nine pieces. Only thirty-five of them were found. He claimed to have thrown the missing pieces into the toilet. It was those body parts that might well have confirmed that the murder had been preceded by a more odious assault. However, when the parts were located, they were in no condition to serve as evidence. As for Ménesclou, he continued to deny that charge.

Following the horrific discovery, a search order was filed and enacted. It would turn out to be a dramatically moving event. The large, angry crowd that had gathered outside the dwelling threatened to lynch the murderer.

At six o'clock, after the arrival of Monsieur Macé and Monsieur Ragon (the investigating magistrate), a fiacre stopped in front of the Deu residence. As Ménesclou got out, a tumultuous roar arose from the crowd.

"Death! Death! Death!" the crowd chanted in unison.

Ménesclou had his hands tied behind his back. He was hatless and his face was sallow. He wore a black, open jacket, an oxford cloth shirt without a tie, a pair of beltless, sagging, black trousers, and ankle boots whose laces were left dangling. He was a dreadful sight to behold, trembling as the officers escorted him inside.

The neighbors were all grouped in the courtyard that he had to traverse. A man who looked to be a strapping and fearless member of the working class stepped forward, clenched is fist and snarled.

"Leave him to me. I'll put a quick end to him!"

"Don't lay a finger on this man," Monsieur Macé said, his face pale as well. "Stay out of the way. He belongs to the law now."

Meanwhile the mother of the poor little victim had come to her doorstep with her youngest child in her arms. She screamed tearfully, "Avenge my daughter! Kill the wretch! Kill him, I say!"

She was comforted by neighbors and led back inside where she fainted dead away.

It is wholly understandable that although Ménesclou's attorneys underscored his youth in their defense, the jury refused to take into consideration a call for mitigating circumstances. He was condemned to death.

President Grévy was of a mind to commute the sentence, but when the female workers in the Gros-Caillou tobacco factories got wind of it, they threatened to take to the streets if Ménesclou's head didn't fall.

Under public pressure, the death warrant was finally signed. The execution was carried out the 7th of September, 1880. It was the last execution I witnessed in Paris.

CHAPTER THIRTY-TWO
The Execution of Louis Ménesclou
(7 September 1880)

At five: thirty in the morning on September 7th, four-year-old Louisette Deu was finally avenged. Ménesclou's head fell just as the sun was rising.

For nearly two weeks a crowd had been milling about the Place de la Roquette. Many spent the entire night there in hopes of getting a good view of the execution that had been announced as imminent. It wasn't until dawn that the throng of guillotine vultures disbanded, only to return again after nightfall.

On the fateful day, as chance would have it, an extremely violent storm broke out at the precise moment that people were about to set off for the Place de la Roquette. They reasoned that the execution would surely not take place in such bad weather. As a consequence, there were no more than fifty onlookers when I arrived on the scene at two o'clock in the morning.

The execution site had taken on a forebodingly sinister aura. The rain had stopped, but flashes of lightning continued to streak across the sky, illuminating in violent, ghostly fashion the tall, black walls of the two prisons, the area surrounding the five stone slabs, and the weapons of the various contingents of troops that arrived the one after the other. All that, the tall denuded walls, the colossal, gray gate through which the prisoner would emerge, the horses, the cavaliers wrapped in their large coats, all that stood out in dazzling silhouettes for just an instant and then fell back into a dense darkness in which only the red glow of lanterns coming and going remained.

Some twenty reporters, representing the major newspapers of Paris, had gathered near the scaffold. All of a sudden we were stupefied but powerless to combat an order from police to move away and join the general public.

We protested vehemently, of course, but our pleas fell on deaf ears. Officers said they had formal orders to keep everyone, especially the press, at a distance from the scaffold. That situation lasted for two hours, until Monsieur Caubet of the Paris police arrived. He reluctantly agreed to receive a representative of the press. That reporter explained that without the presence of the press the execution would appear surreptitious. Caubet ultimately decided to allow access to one reporter per newspaper.

For all that, the view was hardly ideal. We had been relegated to a spot behind a double row of police and infantrymen from the Republican Guard.

Usually it was at three o'clock that we could expect to hear the two heavy vehicles bumping along the Rue de la Folie-Regnault, the one carrying the guillotine and the other for transporting the cadaver to the cemetery. This time it appears that the executioner had overslept. He didn't arrive until four: ten. In order to catch up, he, his aides, and two carpenters began the assembly process in great haste. Haste makes waste, as the saying goes. We could hear one of the aides say, "It's not working." Evidently, the crew was unable to level the quadrangle of brown beams that serve to support the mechanism. The lunette was out of kilter and would not close properly. The blade, in which the executioner had such confidence, refused to slide unimpeded down the grooves. In brief, the crew had to adjust, shift, reset bolts and file edges for more than a quarter of an hour.

The executioner, in order to save time, decided to go to the prison before the assembly was complete, leaving behind an aide to solve the problem of the malfunctioning blade. All the while that the condemned man was being prepared, the aide was absorbed in orchestrating the task, raising the blade and letting it fall, time and time again, and making adjustments with the precision of a musician tuning a violin.

Ménesclou had fallen into a profound state of depression. For the last few days he held out no hope that his sentence would be commuted. He stopped eating and could not sleep. At midnight, however, his spirits seemed to lift. Through the small, cell window that was pounded by the downpours, he could see the lightning bolts streak across the sky. He turned to one of the guards and, trying to smile, said, "Well, it won't be for today. The weather is too bad. So I guess I'll go to sleep." He got undressed. His head had hardly hit the pillow when he fell into a deep sleep.

At five minutes after five, authorities arrived outside his cell: the warden, Monsieur Monsin from security (standing in for Monsieur Macé), accompanied by the usual participants. Ménesclou was still asleep. He was lying on his back and snoring. His arms were draped over the sides of the bed.

He had to be shaken four times before waking up. He sat up at last and looked about quite confused. The clerk read the rejection of his appeal and request for clemency in a very loud voice owing to the young man's partial deafness. During the reading, Ménesclou tried desperately to make sense of what was happening. His entire soul seemed to be reflected in his wide, gaping eyes. His hearing was impaired but his comprehension was not. He gasped, "My God! My God!"

Those were the only words he uttered. He sat silently while Father Crozes endeavored to console him. He didn't protest when he was dressed, restrained, and the collar of his shirt was cut away. He gulped down a glass of wine, and the group began the trek through the prison.

At five: twenty-seven the prison gate opened wide. The gendarmes had already removed their sabers from their sheaths. The blade had been hoisted. Everything was ready. It was fully daylight now.

The executioner led the way, seeming perfectly indifferent, his long arms swaying. Then Father Crozes appeared, followed by the prisoner assisted by two aides. The other aides followed at the rear.

Ménesclou walked steadfastly. It was an astonishing thing to see. Since leaving his cell his face had grown increasingly pale as he approached death, to the point that he seemed transfigured. His ghostly whiteness contrasted flagrantly with his black hair. Yet, though somewhat drawn, his eyes continued to shine. They were flitting right and left as in a state of hallucination, and his head turned with them.

The murderer appeared to be seeing strange and mysterious things, the sort of things brought on by looking into the eyes of death. It wasn't animal fear that his face reflected at that moment. It was rather a form of ecstatic terror, if those two words can be used in tandem. Just then, from the far end of the square near the Rue Servan, a rather high-pitched voice strained with emotion sang out in bravado fashion the title words of an insanely popular song: "Tiens, voilà Mathieu!"[80] No matter how steeled one might be, such a prank, at such a time, is totally disheartening.

Ménesclou was on the scaffold, next to the bascule. As Father Crozes gave him a kiss, the coat that had been thrown over his shoulders was taken away. Stripped to the waist now, his skin was covered with red blotches. The prisoner asked for one last kiss. Then the bascule swung into position and the lunette clicked into place, followed by the sound of the blade falling and the inevitable thud that one can never forget. The head and body were rushed to the waiting vehicle. The scaffold was rinsed clean of blood.

I recall a rather curious theory I heard the former executioner, Monsieur Roch, expound one day.

"When a condemned man is terribly afraid," he said, "there is very little blood. The contrary is true when he dies bravely."

If that's the case, Ménesclou must have been courageous until the end. He lost nearly a half-bucket of blood.

As the cortege was about to leave for the Ivry cemetery, an incident was narrowly averted. The white horse that had transported Father Crozes in the number 148 fiacre since the Franco-Prussian War was changed in favor of a high-spirited bay. It was frightened by all the paraphernalia of human justice and began to lunge about. It took all the skill the driver could summon to regain control of the animal and get it headed in the right direction.

---

[80] "Tiens, voilà Mathieu" ("Well, here's Mathieu") is a song written by singer/lyricist Louis Gabillaud (1846-1899). It was all the rage at the time.

The customary prayers at the Ivry cemetery were quickly said. The medical school had claimed the body, but by some quirk of fate the prefecture had not received the necessary paperwork.

Doctor Sappey, who was present, rushed to Monsieur Caubet's office, but it was already too late for a rather curious experiment he had planned. He wanted to inject the still-warm cadaver with the blood of two young dogs in order to see whether he could reestablish circulation for a few seconds.

Out of necessity the autopsy had to be postponed until one o'clock in the afternoon. In the interim the cadaver had been returned to the coffin.

Following the execution I wanted to visit both the parents of the victim and the parents of the murderer. I went first to the Deu family residence where the crime had been committed, that is to say at 155 Rue de Grenelle.

When I arrived, Madame Deu was on her doorstep chatting with a neighbor. She was speaking quite elatedly and kept repeating, "It's over! It's over!"

Her neighbor asked whether Ménesclou's parents had attended the execution. "I don't think so," Madame Deu said matter-of-factly, "but it was their right."

Almost all of the neighbors had gone to the Place de la Roquette to witness the execution. Of course given the crowd, they weren't able to see anything, but they were all talking about the experience anyway.

At noon, when I arrived at the residence, the Ménesclous were still unaware that their son had been guillotined that morning. They had to read about it in the evening newspapers. The father, who worked in the office of the finance ministry, had gone into work as usual. The mother also went to work at the tobacco factory.

Because she was an esteemed, longtime employee, the director threatened to fire on the spot anyone who made even the slightest allusion to her misfortune. It was the same for her husband at the ministry.

I experienced a great deal of difficulty running down the Ménesclous' address. They had lived at 155 Rue de Grenelle. The day after the crime they left that residence never to return. Initially, they rented a room in a hotel. It wasn't until a week later, and after a difficult search, that they found lodging at 82 Rue de la Fédération, near the Champ-de-Mars: two small rooms at two hundred francs rent per month.

The house itself was a garish sight to see. It was painted completely in red, and the décor could well have served for a performance at the Ambigu-Comique Theater. The parents live a sad life there, known only as Monsieur and Madame Louis.

Their next door neighbor, Madame Henry, is a very kindhearted woman. She is virtually the only person to know of their misfortune, and she has done everything to console them. She told me that the last time the couple visited their son was Saturday afternoon. The condemned man confided his feelings to them that day. "You see," he said, "I just want to get it over one way or the other."

It was so painful for those good people who never stopped loving their son, the murderer.

I am sad to have to add an epilogue to this story. Madame Ménesclou, under the weight of remorse and shame, has lost her mind. She is now interned in the Sainte-Anne psychiatric facility in the 14th arrondissement.

CHAPTER THIRTY-THREE
The Forty Days Misconception

Ménesclou's execution was the last one I witnessed in Paris. Three years have gone by and the scaffold has been erected only once–in Versailles.

That has provided ample respite for me to research a popular misconception that continues to exist despite all efforts to combat it: that is to say, the famous legend of the specific requirement of a forty-day hiatus between the issuing of the death warrant and the enactment of the execution. The newspapers have done their best to disabuse the public of the notion–to no avail whatsoever.

[In this chapter Grison presents a host of statistical information supporting his case. Whereas his research is admirable in a sense, for the modern reader the information itself is of little interest, especially since capital punishment no longer exists in France. It was for him what one might term a pet peeve. In the interest of brevity and congruity, therefore, I have deemed it wise to abridge the chapter and retain only the conclusion, which itself serves as an abstract. F.G.H.]

Thus, in Paris, the city where such matters function with the most regularity, the forty-day hiatus has never existed. Out of more than two hundred executions, I note only two that took place exactly forty days after the death warrant was issued.

So the facts in the matter are indisputable, are they not? Of course that won't prevent some readers from disagreeing, even after having examined the overwhelming evidence I have presented. "He doesn't know what he's talking about," they'll say. "Of course there is a hiatus of forty days."

CHAPTER THIRTY-FOUR
The Patricide of Pierre Lantz
(31 March 1882)

Even with the current trend of granting clemency to virtually everyone, the execution of Pierre Lantz was an exceptional case.

An exceptional case is too little to say. Lantz was the sort of monster that, fortunately for all of us, is quite rare. Because some time has passed since his crime and memory is what it is, I would do well to recapitulate briefly.

Pierre Lantz belonged by birth to the land whose loss we have been lamenting for twelve years–a land so genuinely French that, despite similarities of manners and language, cannot abide German domination. He was born in Lixheim in the Meurthe-et-Moselle region of Lorraine. After having opted for French nationality in 1872, he served in the army for five years. He then set out for America. When he came back, he was just as miserable as when he left. For the next several years he found nothing better to do than to taunt and mistreat his father, a poor, old man who was forced to summon the authorities on numerous occasions in response to the brutality of his indignant son.

"I'll have his skin before it's over," he was quoted as saying. The neighbors who witnessed the scandalous scenes that occurred almost daily were fearful that just such a tragedy would ultimately play out. And indeed it did. On the night of the 15th and 16th of December, 1880, Monsieur Nesling, a foundry worker who lived at the same residence, heard threats, cries, and the sound of a body falling to the floor, followed by a struggle in the hallway. He was on his way out to alert authorities when he saw Pierre Lantz bent over his father and slamming his head against the wall. The father was begging for mercy. Things seemed to settle down, but Pierre Lantz spent the entire night singing loud enough for neighbors to hear.

The following morning, the father's nephew and wife (the Bonsings) came to visit. They found the old man battered, bruised, and bleeding from the beating. He described the scene from the night before and told them that once his son had him on the floor, he tried to do all sorts of odious things to him. The son had left, finally, but only after having taken from him the little money he had.

The next day, which was a Friday, Madame Bonsing returned to the residence to take some milk to the elder Lantz. She found the outer door locked, but managed to get it open. Inside, however, she was unable to open the door to his room. She went outside and peered through a ground-floor window. She saw no one. The bed curtains were drawn. On the window seat she saw a pair of gray trousers and a scarf, both belonging to Pierre. A pillowcase stained with blood lay nearby. She walked away to gather her thoughts. When she returned to the window she saw that the trousers and scarf had disappeared, and the pillowcase had been placed on the table.

It was about nine o'clock in the morning. On her way home Madame Bonsing ran into the mayor and two other men, Kluss, a day laborer, and Stricker, the supervisor of roadways. She told them what had happened. They said they had just seen Pierre walking along the route leading to the border with a package tucked under his arm.

Together they were able to get into the old man's room. They discovered his body which was still warm. It was covered with bruises and showed signs of strangulation, as well as two broken ribs. They also found evidence of the odious crime against nature mentioned earlier that cannot be designated in any language.

Pierre Lantz had gone to France to demand refuge from his sister in Paris. Demand is indeed the word, for he threatened to kill her if she refused. His sister would have none of it. She had him arrested.

Pierre Lantz denied the crime in the beginning. But he had everything and everyone against him, notably his brother, a courageous member of the artillery corps, who gave evidence against him in an outburst of emotion:

"My brother is a coward and a miserable wretch. I hope the court will show him no more mercy than he showed our poor father!"

Lantz was condemned to death, of course. His attorney, however, discovered a legal loophole, and Lantz had to be retried in France. French jurors were just as horrified as the German jurors had been. The result was the same: a sentence of death for patricide. That explains how his execution came to be carried out in Versailles.

I was of course familiar with the execution site in Versailles. I had witnessed the execution of Ange-Valentin Roux there, the eighteen-year-old ruffian who had strangled an elderly woman in Argenteuil. Then it was the month of June beneath a splendid sky. Yesterday morning, however, rain fell in torrents from a blackened sky. It was an eerie spate of weather for an eerie event for those who were awake to see it. For those in the know, it was about to be the first time in six years that it rained on execution day.

But wouldn't you know it, at about three: thirty the clouds dissipated, the stars appeared the one after the other on the horizon, and the rain stopped. So it was a magnificently clear night when I came through Chantiers gate and arrived at Colbert Bridge.

The first light of day illuminated a lovely setting. On one side there was Buc Woods with its narrow trails that disappeared mysteriously into the foliage. To the right stood an old wall next to the military silage storehouse where an alert had been sounded earlier. Another wretch, a Belgian named Boulanger, had sought to take out his revenge on the justice system by setting fire to a haystack. Close by, to the rear, lay the old Porchefontaine Racetrack, beyond which one could see a train puffing along, its engine spitting a fiery stream of light in the dusky distance.

And, in terrible contrast, in the middle of all that, above the left-side walkway along the road to Jouy, above a grassy area covered with daisies and little blue flowers, rose the guillotine, surrounded by ladders, baskets, and the rest of the executioner's deadly paraphernalia.

He was there also, Monsieur Deibler, pale, agitated, impatient, nervous, on edge, to use a common expression. It was a trying time when he needed to do everything possible to avoid any controversy whatsoever that might ignite criticism of the supreme act of justice. The least little misstep might well fuel another avalanche of calls to abolish the death penalty. Despite the lapse of time, antagonists recalled vividly the case of Claude Montcharmont.[81]

His concern was such that Monsieur Deibler had gone to see Monsieur Charles Baudat, the central police commissioner, in an effort to have intimidating reporters kept away from the immediate site. In his wisdom, the commissioner assigned a space for reporters where they could see but that would not allow the troublesome ones to interfere in any way.

Measures to preserve order were admirably implemented, I must say. Two companies from the 2nd regiment of the corps of engineers formed a ring that kept spectators generally at bay. Squads of police from Versailles handled individual fracases. The road above and below was barricaded by two contingents of cuirassiers. From behind hedges and through the foliage curious

---

[81] In May of 1851, Claude Montcharmont, a poacher, was convicted of killing a gendarme and a rural policeman. On execution day he fought the executioners tooth and nail, a struggle that lasted nearly an hour. His cries for help all but incited the crowd to intervene in his behalf. He had to be returned to his cell to wait until reinforcements could be brought in. When he reappeared, his clothes were in shreds and patches of skin were missing from his back. Consequently, Charles Hugo (Victor Higo's son) published an article in *L'Évévenement* critical of the execution. He was arrested and prosecuted for "outrage aux lois" (lack of respect for the law). He was defended on June 11th by none other than his father, Victor, who used his eloquence to attack the death penalty itself. Charles was ultimately found guilty, sentenced to six months incarceration at the Conciergerie, and was fined 500 francs. This and other such happenings caused journalists to be seen as potential foes. Over time, efforts increased to exclude them to the extent possible.

men, women, and children peered at the silhouette of the guillotine in the half-light. They had already been waiting several hours.

Somewhat reassured, Monsieur Deibler climbed into a vehicle at four:thirty and headed for Saint-Pierre prison where the prisoner had been incarcerated for seventy-eight days. There he met Monsieur Vallée, director of the Seine-et-Oise prison system, Monsieur Masson, head guard, Monsieur Durand, police commissioner of the Canton du Nord, Doctor Berrigny, and Pastor Passa, who was assigned to assist the prisoner since he was a member of the Protestant religion.

Pierre Lantz occupied cell number four. According to Monsieur Masson, he had been brutally insolent and prone to rebellion. However, for the last few days he had become more sociable because, like so many before him, he believed that his sentence would be commuted. He drank and ate well, spent the entire day reading, and slept the night through. Seeking to avoid problems on the eve of his execution, Monsieur Masson had the prisoner placed in a straightjacket, where upon guards were met with invectives and threats.

Lantz was sleeping when officials arrived at his cell at eight minutes after five. Monsieur Passa was assigned to wake him. He did so as gently as possible. The prisoner shuddered. After a few seconds he opened his eyes.

"My poor Lantz," the pastor said, "the mercy of God is all that remains for you, for the justice of man has come to claim you."

Lantz sat up abruptly. He looked around frantically and fell back on his bed. Doctor Berrigny feared that he might pass out. He grasped the prisoner's arm and took his pulse. "It's just a reflex reaction," he said. "There's nothing to it."

The pastor spoke to the condemned man in a soft, encouraging voice. With his straightjacket removed, Lantz calmed down and began to get dressed. The pastor continued speaking to him and reciting prayers for the dying. The prisoner listened attentively.

Given his disposition, his reactions were quite surprising. The head guard and doctor were visibly moved.

"I'm ready," he said simply when Monsieur Passa had finished.

Preparations were quickly administered. All condemned prisoners have their hair cut and are shaved clean beforehand. The sole task that remained was to cut away the shirt collar. Despite all the precautions that had been taken, when the scissors touched the prisoner's neck, Lantz threw his head back and thrust his arms and legs outward.

In his soft, warm voice, the pastor asked, "Would you like a cordial, a bit of rum or cognac with sugar?"

"No, thank you, I don't want anything."

"You see, my dear Lantz," the pastor continued, "Monsieur Masson has not held your behavior yesterday against you."

"Please forgive me, Monsieur, I'm quick-tempered, I am sorry."

Monsieur Masson shook his hand, as did the other guards. The contingent left the prison and got into the vehicle. A plank had been fitted transversally toward the front to form a bench. The prisoner and the pastor sat down. The aides sat in the rear. Monsieur Deibler sat up front beside the driver. The vehicle pulled away.

We reporters were waiting along the roadway leading to the bridge, in the middle of the ring formed by the troops and opposite the guillotine. The rays of dawning sunshine softened the lines of the death machine, turning it a tawny brown, and tinged the underside of clouds with a coppery hue. In response, idyllically, the little birds awoke in the hedgerows and greeted us with their morning songs.

At six o'clock the Chantiers gate, which had been closed to keep the crowd away, was opened to allow the cortege to pass. Just as the vehicle and accompanying mounted gendarmes were coming through, a hoard of thrill-seeking street urchins streamed around them and darted under the horses, at the risk of being trampled, in order to blend into the crowd and avoid pursuing soldiers.

The cuirassiers closed ranks and the gendarmes covered the flanks opposite the guillotine. The vehicle stopped twenty-five meters from the scaffold, the twenty-five meters that the law mandated that those found guilty of parricide walk barefoot, their heads covered with a black veil and cloaked in a shirt.

Lantz was so attired. He had the black veil over his head and wore a long shirt, or rather a peignoir, over his jacket and trousers. He climbed down slowly from the vehicle. He shivered when his bare feet touched the icy ground. He moved forward without incident, nevertheless, with an aide on one side of him and, on the other side, the pastor with whom he talked as he went along. The prisoner walked as steadfastly as the restraints on his legs would allow. Monsieur Deibler was walking toward the guillotine now; he seemed less assured, however.

The peignoir and veil were removed. Lantz shared a final kiss with the pastor. After looking around, his eyes rose and focused on the guillotine. He took a step toward the scaffold, but Monsieur Chaussier, the criminal court bailiff, stopped him in order to read the death warrant.

"No, no," the pastor interjected, "It's useless to prolong this man's agony. The document is four pages long." He patted the prisoner on the shoulder. "Isn't that right, Lantz, you waive the right to have the warrant read, don't you?"

"Yes, yes," the prisoner assented with a nod.

Upon a sign from Monsieur Grison, the registry clerk, the bailiff relented and walked away. Lantz remained calm. He asked Monsieur Passa for one more kiss.

That scene seemed to take forever. What seemed longer still was the space of time it took for Monsieur Deibler to take the prisoner by the shoulders, position him gently on the bascule just the way he wanted him–as though he were a coiffeur making a valued client comfortable in a hairdressing chair–before deciding to reach up and release the blade. That took over a minute, not the usual fifteen seconds to which we had grown accustomed.

But, finally, the thing was done!

The funeral vehicle containing the body was about to head off toward Gonards cemetery, escorted by Monsieur Chauvin from the Canton du Sud. The crowd, having been kept back until then, surged forth, avid to see the bloody remains. As for me, I began the trek back to Versailles. A strange thing: just as I was passing through the Chantiers gate, the sky darkened and the rain began to fall once again.

The chief of staff at the Versailles hospital had requisitioned the body for the purpose of experimentation.

After having been inhumed, the body was retrieved and taken to the hospital.

What could those experiments have produced? Very little, I should think, given that the body had to be transported to the cemetery to be buried and then exhumed. Certainly not as much as the experiments on cadavers performed immediately following the execution, as in the case of Prunier at Beauvais, for example.

CHAPTER THIRTY-FIVE
Conclusion: The Scale of Penalties

I am bringing this book to a close at the beginning of 1883 at a time when a year has passed without a single execution. The number of commutations granted currently demonstrates amply that it won't be long before the death penalty will be legally abolished, if, indeed, that has not already occurred in point of fact. As a consequence, I believe it necessary to conclude with some thoughts on the present-day shortcomings of crime control.

Capital punishment has numerous adversaries. Some of them have gone so far as to try to assist murderers to flee in order to avoid the guillotine. Each time La Roquette prison welcomes another condemned prisoner, philanthropists begin their campaign anew.

Among the many arguments they present in their defense, they use one that has been very effective: they cite the youth of murderers. That argument saved Gilles and Abadie, the Montreuil murderers, just as it had saved Perrot and Barré a few months before and would save Bistor and Foullois, among others.[82]

"They are so young," they say, "you don't want to commit the barbarism of killing children, do you?"

---

[82] For Gilles and Abadie see the beginning of Chapter One. Charles Perrot was sentenced to death for the murder of his grandparents in Auxerre (30 September 1878). His accomplice was sentenced to prison in perpetuity. For Bistor and Foullois see the opening paragraph of Chapter One.

As far as I'm concerned, it's precisely their youth that supports the antithesis. I would be more inclined to pardon an elderly person worn by life, embittered by long years of sterile endeavor, of fruitless labor, of woes merited or unmerited, hardened by misfortune, envious of others, seeking once and for all a balm for all his suffering in a crime that is for him a form of retaliation.

I have no pity for those precocious monsters, like Gilles, who speak of their crimes with an angelic smile on their pink lips, whose cheeks glow with pride when the refinement of their cruelties is detailed and when society condemns the viciousness of their acts. They are bourgeoning flowers, if you like, but flowers whose buds begin to rot on the stem from their very first growth and who need to be culled if you wish to save the garden.

They are children, you say. Well, listen to those children.

"The old lady was easy to kill, but the old man was tough." That was Perrot speaking about his grandmother and his grandfather. "When we finished," he continued, "we went to the henhouse. I had grown cold waiting for the 'moment' to arrive. I had become hoarse. I ate raw eggs to clear my voice. There's nothing like it. And then we made a flaming brandy drink. I had blood on my hands. As I held them above the flame they smelled like blood sausage."

My heart bursts at hearing such horrors. My pen refuses to write, and you say these children should be spared for redemption?

No, for those criminals and many others there is no repentance. They are not capable of it. Why? Because they have no conscience. That sense has completely atrophied. That sort of baby feels nothing when killing a man, even if it's his father. There is no emotion whatsoever. I've seen them up close during my ten years of covering their crimes as a reporter; I've heard them outside the offices of investigating magistrates. When they thought they were out of sight and out of earshot, they laughed, they joked, they talked of their chances for salvation–salvation for them meant getting off scot-free, don't forget it!

"I'm too young," they tell themselves, and that's why they get started before turning twenty, in order to avoid the guillotine. That's why we now have so many young murderers. If we added them up, it would be terrifying. In the space of a few years, we had the three murderers from Argenteuil, setting out on a lark from Versailles to kill an old woman, robbing and thieving as they went and, once the crime had been committed, joyously playing a game of cards over her dying body. They were seventeen and eighteen years old. We had the aforementioned Perrot and Barré who also traveled on foot to slaughter Perrot's grandparents, all the way from Paris to Auxerre, some eighty kilometers. We had young Olivier, a promising young fellow, who bludgeoned his cousin to death with a rolling pin and tried to deflect suspicion with a Machiavellian astuteness worthy of an "old war horse." We had Félix Lemaître, the fourteen-year-old apprentice who disemboweled a six-year-old boy to "see how it felt."[83] We had Fallois. We had Ménesclou. If we looked further, we would surely uncover more such cases, for the provinces have their share of young murderers.

---

[83] That murder took place in Paris in 1881.

So, in general, I don't have more pity for young murderers than for the others. For all of them the death penalty is a horrible necessity, but it is a necessity.

It's not out of love of blood or for the repulsive and imposing spectacle of capital execution that I support the application of the death penalty. It's because, after having witnessed so much, after having discussed the matter at length, after having weighed all the reasons for and against, I have arrived at the conclusion that, whatever its worth, it's the only deterrent we have for murderers. By murderers I mean *professional murderers*. The others, whom I call *situational murderers*, are those that are motivated to kill by anger, passion, hatred, or revenge. For no threat–be it being burned alive or drawn and quartered–will deter them.

Here is what is strange. Situational murderers are less likely to have their sentences commuted. The public has no pity for them. Thus, in 1879 for example, the President of the Republic had a choice of Achille Lequette, Augustin Martin, and Théotime Prunier, all of whom had been condemned to death. He gave reprieves to the first two who were professional highwaymen, retaining the death penalty for Prunier's act of drunken folly, the rape (two times) of a cadaver.

If I had a preference, it would be for such extraordinary criminals that I would reserve pity. Those are the ones I would spare.

Suppose that Billoir had never been brought to justice. I would bet one hundred to one that, for the rest of his life, he would not have harmed a hair on anyone's head.

Suppose that Gilles and Abadie had been set free. Within two weeks they would have killed someone else.

Some people claim that the death penalty prevents no crime. They are totally wrong. Just to cite one example, there is an entire class of criminals whose specialty is entering apartment buildings and opening doors at random. If no one is at home, they ransack and pillage the apartment. If they find someone at home, they simply offer their apologies for their mistake, and they move on to the next apartment.

Now, those criminals are usually ex-convicts. Many are inveterate lawbreakers. Some are on the run from the police. They know that if they are caught, they will face forced labor. Let's suppose that the death penalty is abolished. They will say:

If I'm arrested, it will be forced labor.
If I kill someone, it will be forced labor.
If I kill, I can escape.
If I kill, there is no greater risk, and I can always escape.
Therefore, I shall not hesitate to kill.
And they will kill.
Without fail.

At present, the prospect of being guillotined prevents ten murders a day in Paris. So if you decide to abolish the death penalty, I'll go along with it, but on the condition that it will be replaced by another penalty that will protect us.

I view the penal code as a means of preventing wrongdoing rather than a means of punishing wrongdoing. It's not vengeance that I seek. It is rather a means of striking fear in the hearts of those who are tempted by misdeeds.

By executing murderers I seek to restrain by fear those who are tempted to imitate them. It is a barbarous act, I admit, but the life of a murderer is not worth the life of an honest man. As the old saying goes, "I'd rather kill the devil than have him kill me."

Thus, if you can find an effective, bloodless deterrent, I'm all for it, enthusiastically so.

But forced labor does not fill the bill. If you only knew how criminals mock it, how laughable they find it!

Ah, when there were the old fashioned work camps, those hideous work camps, with the chains, the convicts coupled together two by two, dragging their shackles, exposed to public scorn, assigned the most odious tasks on the docks, in the stinking muck, led about like so many beasts of burden and subject to the overseer's truncheon . . . . Yes, there was fear of that.

But now, like Sganarelle, we've change all that.[84] We have work camps bathed in rose water, work camps where everyone is family. The decree of 27 March 1852, followed by the law of 30 May 1854, have set us straight.

No more work, no more chains. The convicts are free. It's just a matter of changing climes.

Out of paternal compassion, the air of Guiana has been deemed too unhealthy. So the penal colony in Guiana has been eliminated for continental convicts. They are now sent to New Caledonia where conditions are much more suitable. They are given land, they are given tools, they are given seed and subsidies–that is to say,

---

[84] The reference is to Molière's comedy, *Sganarelle or the Imaginary Cuckold*. Sganarelle's entire outlook is based on mistaken assumptions that lead him hilariously astray.

everything that the government would never provide free colonists.

Provided that they behave themselves, and that is so easy, they are given permission to marry or have their family come live with them in the colony. They can even become homesteaders on a parcel of land with the capacity to sell for profit their cultivated products on the open market. In other words, they can enjoy, either partially or completely, all the civil rights of the colony. And to add insult to injury, the term *convict* has been eliminated in favor of *transportees*.

Frankly, how do you expect those conditions to strike fear in the hearts of people such as Gilles and Abadie who had to eke out an existence on the streets of Paris and, for the difficulty of it, turned to crime?

And yet, that's the sole punishment that is being proposed to replace the death penalty!

Conversely, there is a punishment that I find much too severe. I'm talking about reclusion. I have seen the conditions of incarcerated prisoners with my own eyes, and I am appalled.

You know the type of life they have to lead. They are absolutely controlled. In their cells, they are fed water and whole meal bread. They are deprived of beer and wine and any soothing drinks. They are expected to maintain complete silence; they are forced to work tirelessly at a very low wage and receive only a quarter of their earnings.

In my life I've seen the most horrifying sights. I've seen bloody cadavers that have been hacked to pieces and disfigured, but for all that, I was unable to keep from shuddering one day in Melun when I saw the gritty faces, bent backs, and the crafty eyes pinched with fear of living beings sentenced to the tomb for five or ten years and who, when they are released, are no more than walking cadavers.

Their suffering is much worse than anything forced labor has to offer. And yet it is rated a degree lower. If you steal, you will be sentenced to prison. If you kill, you'll be sent to New Caledonia. You would have to be stupid or crazy not to kill, you see.

That's the reasoning that runs through the minds of those poor people. I knew of one in Melun who said to the warden one day, "Monsieur, I can't take it here in the provincial prison anymore. I have a brother who is in New Caledonia. He wrote me and said that he's getting along quite well there. I'd like to join him there. Could you arrange it?"

The warden tried to make him understand that it wasn't up to him. But the prisoner insisted.

"Well then," he said, "I'll just have to commit a crime. I'm not really a bad guy, but since there is no other means, I'll have to take it out on someone. I won't kill because I don't want to face the guillotine, but I'll injure someone."

Sure enough, a week later he stabbed his guard in the back with a piece of iron removed from his bedframe and sharpened on the stone floor of his cell. For his efforts, he was sentenced to forced labor in perpetuity.

"Thank you, gentlemen," he replied, "that's exactly what I wanted."

That is often the case. Incarcerated prisoners commit a crime with the sole intent of receiving an aggravated sentence because that means forced labor.

Therefore, if it's the fear of forced labor you hope to use to deter crime, you are sadly mistaken.

And it is also for that precise reason that the death penalty is the only true means of protecting honest people against murderers. It is, in a word, indispensable.

APPENDIX

Documents pertaining to the case of Barré and Lebiez

News of the murder and dismemberment of an aging milk vendor in Paris sent shock waves across Europe and the Atlantic. The heinousness of the crime was in large part responsible for the notoriety, but the moral and philosophical disposition of one of the culprits, Paul Lebiez, attracted interest beyond the attention usually generated by such acts of depravity. Lebiez was a hardened Darwinist and a close reader of Dostoyevsky's *Crime and Punishment*. According to those who wrote about the case, Darwinian theory and the crime depicted in the Russian novel had morphed in Lebiez's mind to the point that he felt obliged to carry out the murder in the name of society. At the time of the murder, 1878, both the theory and the novel were often in the news. *Crime and Punishment* was published in 1866, and the disquieting psychology of its protagonist, Raskolnikoff, was frequently discussed in cafés and literary journals. Darwin's controversial *The Descent of Man* was a mere six years off the presses.

The items that follow document the intenseness and breadth of the interest in the case. The first item contains excerpts from the pages of Henry Brodribb Irving's *Studies of French Criminals in the Nineteenth Century*, published in London by William Heinemann in 1901. Irving's account is moving and well researched. He went so far as to obtain public records and translate them to provide accurate dialogue for his English-reading audience. Three of the four remaining items are articles devoted to the crime and trial that were taken from the pages of English newspapers and published by the *New York Times*. The final item is a translation of the official police report of the double execution of Aimé Barré and Paul Lebiez, signed by the Chief of Police of the City of Paris, Sélim Ansart.

Excerpts from *Studies of French Criminals in the Nineteenth Century*

"That Paul was capable of such an act was proved beyond a doubt within the space of a few weeks. At the root of his character lay a cold and cynical insensibility which, to oblige a friend or serve some temporary need of his own, would stick at nothing. Lacking the energy and enterprise of Barré, he was far less nervous and excitable than his friend; naturally averse to prolonged endeavor of any kind, he was only too ready to have recourse to a prompt and speedy assassination, which to one holding his views on evolution, would be no more than a justifiable incident in the struggle for life. Lebiez's extreme application of the Darwinian hypothesis stood him in good stead as a criminal; it made him coldly insensible to that horror of murder which is engendered in mankind by a belief that they are fashioned in the likeness of a divinity: whilst at the same time it gave him that stoical fortitude of bearing the supreme expiation of his guilt, which an intellectual conviction of some sort goes a long way to sustain." (89-90)

"Lebiez had not seen much of Barré since the murder. He had been very busy. He had been successfully negotiating for his appointment as editor of an advanced radical newspaper that was just being started. On April 11th he delivered a lecture at the Salle d'Arras. He chose as his subject, 'Darwinism and the Church.' He gave full expression to his views on the struggle for life. 'At the banquet of Nature,' he said, 'there is not room, there are not enough covers laid for all the guests; each one struggles to find a place; the strong push out the weak. Hence this struggle for life, family against family, species against species, a civil war without peace or truth, among animals and plants the same.' Religion and Science he declared to be absolutely irreconcilable." (98)

"Lebiez, as a friend and colleague of Barré, had been cognizant of these futile negotiations, and was full of resentment at the unworthy reluctance of the old woman to comply with his friend's harmless request. Her grudging behavior obliged him to regard the situation from the point of view of the struggle for life. He resolved the question of the old woman's right to exist, as Raskolnikoff in Dostoieffsky's great novel decided the fate of the old woman, Alena Ivanovna. 'She's an old miser,' he said to Barré; 'what right has she to hoard up her gold when there are many others who could put it to some use? It's disgusting to see an old woman like that, who sits all day like a bear crouching in her chair, go on piling up a fortune that's no good to anybody.'" (92)

"We had occasion to compare the murder of the old woman Gillet by Barré and Lebiez with that of the old woman Alena Ivanovna by the student Raskolnikoff in Dosteieffsky's novel, *Crime and Punishment*. In the details of the crime the resemblance is startling, and would almost suggest that one of the two assassins was familiar with the Russian novel; the reasoning by which Lebiez justified to Barré the murder of the old miser is precisely that of Raskolnikoff previous to the crime. But between Dostoieffsky's hero and Barré and Lebiez there is a signal difference. Raskolnikoff commits murder under the influence of extreme cerebral excitement, ending in a violent attack of illness, the result of hunger and despair; his reason seems to be temporarily affected by the action of acute physical and mental distress on a highly sensitive temperament. But assassination of the old woman Gillet by Barré and Lebiez is as deliberately planned and coolly executed a murder as any in the annals of crime." (101)

Articles published in *The New York Times*

August 11, 1878

TWO FAST YOUNG MEN MURDER AND CUT UP AN OLD WOMAN FOR HER MONEY
Paris Correspondence of the London Telegraph

One of those great trials which always rivet the attention of the Parisian public, known as the mystery of the Rue Poliveau, came before the Assize Court of the Seine this morning. Although the crime is of comparatively recent date, your readers will doubtless have forgotten the details. Toward the end of last March the inhabitants of a lodging house, in an obscure street in Paris–the Rue Poliveau–which opens on the Boulevard de l'Hôpital, noticed a strangely disagreeable smell. The landlord set about looking for the cause of it, and entered an empty room which had been let six days previously to two young men, who had deposited a package there but had never returned to claim it. The foul odor was suffocating, and a woman opened a cupboard in the wall in which she found a large parcel, carefully wrapped up in tarred paper. On untying it, what was her horror to discover that it contained the thighs and arms of a woman enveloped in blood-stained linen. The whole quarter of the Jardin des Plantes was thrown into consternation, and an inquiry was instituted, but nothing came of it. While all Paris was talking with indignation of the horrible crime, and of the impunity of its authors, it was learned that the friends of a milk-woman, the Widow Gillet, living in the Rue Paradis Poissonnière, had missed her, and had even come to look for her at the Morgue. One of these neighbors knew that the Widow Gillet had a cauterized wound on her left arm. The limb found in the cupboard had such a mark. The remains were at length recognized as those of the Widow Gillet; but the mystery was who had killed her, and for what reasons. She was industrious and economical to a fault, and she had saved 12,000 francs, which were invested in Rentes. She used to boast of her fortune, and let everybody into the secret of its existence. She had more than a limited circle of male acquaintances, and one of these, known to be her lover, was arrested, but released again in a few days. Then the neighbors remembered a certain Aimé Barré, who called himself an agent and was in frequent consultation with the Widow Gillet. After some hesitation, the mistress of the house in the Rue Poliveau recognized Barré as one of the two young men who had hired the room. The inquiry, however, was very long and difficult, but at last Barré avowed his crime, and denounced Lebiez as his accomplice. Barré is the son of honest country folk, whose only ambition was to put their son in a good position. He was placed in a notary's office at Angers, but, unfortunately, made the acquaintance of one Léontine Lepin, a married woman separated from her husband. She became his mistress and persuaded him to go to Paris. The credulous father allowed him to do so on the pretext of completing his studies. Little by little Barré developed his life of idleness and debauchery. He persuaded his father to entrust him with his 20-years' savings, which he spent. He entered the office of a notary, and appropriated several sums of money, by which he was enabled to set up a place of business in the Rue Hauteville. Neither money nor clients came, but only creditors and the bailiffs, at the sight of whom Léontine fled. Barré thus abandoned, gave himself up more and more to criminal designs, and it was at this time that he formed the plan of killing the widow Gillet, who lived a few doors from him and sold milk in his street. Not daring to attack her alone, he enlisted the services of Paul Lebiez, a medical student, who, too, had a mistress, and was pressed for money. This Lebiez was known in the cafés of the Latin Quarter for his violence and socialistic tendencies. The affair was arranged between them. The Widow Gillet was invited to dinner at the Rue Hauteville. When she entered the room Barré struck her on the head and the woman fell; but as she was not dead, Lebiez plunged a *bistouri* into her heart and lungs, in order to cause internal hemorrhage. The following day the corpse was put into a trunk and taken to the house of Lebiez, who cut it in pieces. The arms and thighs were carried to the Rue Poliveau, and the rest of the body was sent in the trunk to Le Mans. Such are the facts which are now before the court. Barré is 25 years of age, Lebiez 24, and Léontine Lepin 25. Barré is a short man with brown hair. He wears a beard and a mustache, and his features are tolerably regular. Lebiez is darker and better-looking than Barré. He is, indeed, quite a fine-looking fellow, with a highly intelligent expression. Léontine Lepin is a vulgar looking, ugly woman; in fact, the only attractive point about her is the agreeable union of brown eyes and brown hair.

The Assize Court was filled as soon as the doors were open, and at 10 o'clock not a place was to be found. It was said in court that the President has received no less than 4,500 applications for tickets, of which 2,000 came from women–indeed, there were quite as many present as there were men. Owing, however, to the advanced period of the season, there were but few of those celebrities who usually grace Parisian criminal trials with their presence. On the table in front of the desk were placed the large trunk which was sent to Le Mans with the body, head, and feet of the corpse; a second box containing things belonging to Léontine Lepin, and other matters. The sitting began at 10:30 o'clock, the Advocate-General De Fourchy representing the State, and Maîtres Georges Lachaud and Demange being the counsel for the accused. Léontine Lepin, who is charged as an accomplice, was represented by Maître Crochard. After swearing in the jury the President proceeded to examine with great ability and tact the two assassins, both of whom failed to show any extraordinary strength of mind. Apart from the moral lessons which the *interrogatoire* usually contains, nothing was brought to light except the facts which have already been indicated. Barré and Lebiez both confess their crime; but from accomplices they have become deadly enemies, their absorbing desire now being to throw the burden of the murder and the shame of its instigation upon each other. The answers of Barré and Lebiez brought out into stronger relief than ever the cold-blooded and horrible nature of their crime.

August 17, 1878

THAT FRENCH MURDER CASE
MYSTERY OF THE RUE POLIVEAU CLEARED UP
From the London Telegraph, Aug. 2

[The first half of this article repeats the content of the August 11th article. The remainder is reproduced below. The reader will surely notice the writer's failure to control the urge to compare the French justice system, unfavorably, to the English justice system.]

Paris has during the past week been greatly excited by a trial of a most extraordinary character.

[. . .] There is much in the trial that to Englishmen, accustomed to a widely different system of criminal procedure, must appear strange. The murder was as brutal a one as could well be conceived, and the two criminals actually admitted their guilt, endeavoring each to throw the guilt on the other. Thus, the learned advocates retained for the defense, instead of making any attempt to break down the case for the prosecution, contented themselves by delivering powerful harangues suggesting extenuating circumstances, and praying for a merciful consideration of the case. What these extenuating circumstances were the summary of the speeches of Maîtres Lachaud and Demange which have appeared sufficiently show. For Barré it was urged by the most eminent advocate at the French Bar that he had become entangled in the clutches of a young woman, a species of *succube*, who had wrecked his life, and that, under her control and at her suggestion, he had committed the crime with which he was charged. Exactly such a speech might have been made in behalf of the unfortunate George Barnwell; but the prosaic English mind would fail to discover any extenuating circumstances in such a case.[85] For Lebiez it was suggested that he ought not to be guillotined because he is an atheist, whereas if his life is spared, he might possibly become a good Roman Catholic and repent him of the error of his ways. The Counsel for Léontine Lepin had an easier task. He had simply to urge that there was no evidence whatsoever that she took any active part in the murder, or was even aware of it until it had been finally committed. The clemency extended to her is reasonable enough. Equally reasonable is it that the two male prisoners should have been left absolutely condemned to the hands of the executioner. It appeared that with the money Barré had derived from his share in the unhappy old woman's assassination he had entered into a partnership with Lebiez for the foundation of a Communistic newspaper. This fact, no doubt, went some way toward sealing the fate of the two principal criminals. To kill an old woman is, no doubt, murder in the contemplation of all law. But there are circumstances under which a sort of extenuation might be found for this or almost any crime in the eyes of a French jury. They are always singularly averse to sentence a culprit to the guillotine, and are always eager to find some point or other in the case on the strength of which they may satisfy themselves that the supreme penalty of the law might with advantage be remitted. If, for instance, a son shoots his father, a French jury may

---

[85] George Barnwell, a character in George Lillo's celebrated play, *The London Merchant* (1731), is a young apprentice who is led astray by a prostitute.

find that the father on his side had behaved harshly to the son, or had not made him sufficiently liberal allowance, or had spoken to him in terms of insult and contumely. In the present case, had Barré been alone it would perhaps have been urged that he was a young man under the influence of a wicked woman, consumed by a passionate affection for her, and not altogether responsible for his acts. To our own English feelings and sentiments such a plea is too repulsive to be calmly considered. In France it would in 9 cases out of 10 pass current. What has sent Barré to the guillotine is that he and Lebiez, his accomplice, instead of being what we might call interesting criminals, were in reality mere assassins, whose object it was to make a few hundreds of francs, and with them to start a radical newspaper. Even French sentiment has its limits, and in the present instance, if there was one thing clearer than another, it was that two more detestable miscreants than Barré and Lebiez have never yet paid the penalty of their crime on the scaffold.

September 23, 1878

THE EXECUTION OF BARRÉ AND LEBIEZ
Paris Correspondence of the London Standard

They were sleeping quietly last night, while a yelling crowd of roughs, and a more repulsive crowd of fashionable youths, reeking from the *cabinets particuliers* of Boulevard cafés and the *boudoirs* of the Quartier Breda, were driving the Police from the stations they had taken up to keep a clear space round the guillotine, which had been built up in the dead of night. A good many were arrested, but the crowd was altogether beyond the control of the Police. For years past there never has been such a throng so close to that hideous instrument of death. Formerly the guillotine was built upon a platform about 8 feet high; now it is level with the ground. The object of this is the charitable one of sparing the poor wretch about to be killed the ordeal of going up a dozen steps. It makes it look doubly hideous. A board is also fixed in front of the two upright posts so as to prevent the condemned man seeing the gleaming knife as he emerges from the prison door.

After two hours of fighting, shouting, yelling in the square outside, the sun shone out dimly through the mist, as the prison clock struck 5:30. The folding doors of the prison were thrown open wide, and a pale figure, supported by a priest on one side and a rough-looking man at the other, hobbled up rapidly close to the guillotine. He then gave a start and fell back one step; the priest held up a crucifix to his lips, he was hurried forward, the knife gleamed like lightning, and it was all over with for Barré–let us hope–but it was not over for the public. Through some mismanagement on his part, or the convulsive movements of the headless body, the executioner failed to turn it over into the coffin awaiting its reception, and while he was trying to force it in the blood kept spouting out as if forced out by a pump. There was a loud cry of horror from the crowd; but immediately after, and as the executioner's men were still dashing water over the platform and wiping the knife, the portals of the prison again opened to give passage to Lebiez. He was ghastly pale, but evidently more firm and collected than the other; he looked at the guillotine without a quiver, kissed the crucifix, said in a loud voice, "Adieu," and the rest followed. Some man in the crowd shouted "Bravo Lebiez," several more fainted, and those who did not experienced a very uncomfortable feeling, and certainly wished themselves away. I have no desire to dwell on the scandalous and ruffianly scenes that attended this double execution. But I fully echo the wish expressed tonight by the *Temps*, that the present mode of carrying out capital punishment should be altered. As at present conducted, it is a mere gratification for the lowest instincts of the criminal population.

Paris, 10 September 1878

Prefecture of Police

National Police Report 11920

The execution of the prisoners named Barré and Lebiez, which took place the day before yesterday, attracted to the Place de la Roquette and the surrounding area a crowd that cannot be estimated at less than 25 to 30,000 individuals.[86]

Public curiosity, stimulated by the sensational articles of a certain newspaper, had reached such a degree that for the past week, at midnight, a large number of people had been assembling in the vicinity of the Condemned Prisoners Facility and had not left until they

---

[86] It is likely that the report was filed on the tenth of September but written on the ninth, for both Grison and the public record list the execution date as the seventh of September.

were convinced no preparations were being made for the execution.

I attended the execution of the two prisoners named Barré and Lebiez, as I have attended all those that have taken place since 1871. I had never seen such a large crowd; never had I discerned such a frenzy, such a fevered pitch on the part of the public.

The crowd was so turbulent that The Corps of Police, which had been organized with care and dispatch, experienced great difficulty in carrying out assignments. The crowd pressed ever forward in an effort to gain a better vantage point near the barriers that had been set up for the occasion.

The barriers had been placed at such a great distance from the execution site that even those who managed to gain the front rows could see almost nothing. Nevertheless, there was no end of pushing, shoving, shouting, and, sometimes, singing. It was an event that invited disorder and the exchange of the grossest of jokes and pranks.

Alongside the public at large, which we were finally able to control, it is necessary to point out a category of people that grows larger and larger with each execution: they are the privileged spectators, or those who believe they should be.

I am not talking about the journalists, whose presence is explicable–even though their numbers have grown larger than suitable. I am talking about a swarm of people demanding to be allowed as close as possible to the scaffold, citing bona fide rights or producing identification cards or letters of recommendation.

At yesterday's execution the number of such people was quite high. Not all of them were allowed inside the barriers, it is true, but the number of them admitted was large enough to hamper the proceedings.

I shall note in passing this detail that is not without interest in enabling officials to understand the nature of a segment of the public attracted to executions.

As soon as word spreads in Paris that an execution is imminent, all the late-night diners at fashionable restaurants, males and females alike, all the stragglers in the establishments that are grudgingly allowed late closings, in a word, all the licentious idlers that a city like Paris can accommodate, are attuned and have taken measures to receive last-minute updates. The vagabonds all leave their usual haunts and come to gather around the Place de la Roquette.

I consider it a shameful and deplorable reality that this thirst for sensationalism has invaded every level of society. The crowd of people leaving the Place de la Roquette takes away nothing more than unsettling impressions of disgust or the regret that its need for the lurid has not been satisfied. Was that the goal of legislators who had hoped to find in capital punishment a means of curtailing immorality?

Given these conditions, I believe it is time to modify the legislation by abolishing public executions and by adopting a program of executions within the walls of a prison, as certain other countries have implemented.

I do not doubt that public opinion would welcome a reform that positions taken in the press have prepared these last few days.

Sélim Ansart
Chief of the Municipal Police of Paris

FRENCH MYSTERIES & THRILLERS

M. Allain & P. Souvestre. *The Daughter of Fantômas*
A. Anicet-Bourgeois & Lucien Dabril. *Rocambole*
A. Bernède. *Belphegor*; *Judex* (w/Louis Feuillade); *The Return of Judex* (w/Louis Feuillade); *The Shadow of Judex* (anthology)
A. Bisson & G. Livet. *Nick Carter vs. Fantômas*
V. Darlay & H. de Gorsse. *Arsène Lupin vs. Sherlock Holmes: The Stage Play*
Séamas Duffy. *Sherlock Holmes in Paris*
Paul Féval. *The Black Coats (The Parisian Jungle; Heart of Steel; The Sword-Swallower; 'Salem Street; The Invisible Weapon; The Companions of the Treasure; The Cadet Gang); Gentlemen of the Night; John Devil*
Émile Gaboriau. *Monsieur Lecoq*
Goron & Émile Gautier. *Spawn of the Penitentiary*
Paul d'Ivoi. *Around the World on Five Sous* (w/Henri Chabrillat)
Rick Lai. *Shadows of the Opera: Retribution in Blood; Sisters of the Shadows: The Curse of Cagliostro*
Steve Leadley. *Sherlock Holmes: The Circle of Blood*
Maurice Leblanc. *Arsène Lupin vs. Countess Cagliostro; Arsène Lupin vs. Sherlock Holmes (1. The Blonde Phantom; 2. The Hollow Needle); The Island of the Thirty Coffin; 813; The Many Faces of Arsène Lupin* (anthology)
Gaston Leroux. *Chéri-Bibi; The Phantom of the Opera; Rouletabille & the Mystery of the Yellow Room; Rouletabille at Krupp's*
Richard Marsh. *The Complete Adventures of Judith Lee*
William Patrick Maynard. *The Terror of Fu Manchu; The Destiny of Fu Manchu*
Frank J. Morlok. *Sherlock Holmes: The Grand Horizontals; Sherlock Holmes vs Jack the Ripper*
Jean Petithuguenin. *The Adventures of Ethel King*
Antonin Reschal. *The Adventures of Miss Boston*
P. de Wattyne & Y. Walter. *Sherlock Holmes vs. Fantômas*
David White. *Fantômas in America*
Pierre Yrondy. *The Adventures of Thérèse Arnaud*

www.ingramcontent.com/pod-product-compliance
Lightning Source LLC
Chambersburg PA
CBHW030136170426
43199CB00008B/92